A Practical Guide for Policy Analysis

A Practical Guide for Policy Analysis

The Eightfold Path to More Effective Problem Solving

Second Edition

Eugene Bardach

Richard and Rhoda Goldman School of Public Policy
University of California, Berkeley

CQ PRESS

A Division of Congressional Quarterly Inc.
Washington, D.C.

CQ Press
2300 N Street, N.W., Suite 800
Washington, D.C. 20037

202-729-1900; toll-free, 1-866-4CQ-PRESS (1-866-427-7737)

www.cqpress.com

♾ The paper used in this publication exceeds the requirements of the American National Standard for Information Sciences—Permanence of Paper for Printed Library Materials, ANSI Z39.48-1992.

Printed and bound in the United States of America

11   10   09   08   07   6   7   8   9   10

Cover and interior design by Auburn Associates, Inc.

RAND Corporation is gratefully acknowledged for granting permission to reprint the content in Appendix A, previously published in J. P. Caulkins et al., "Mandatory Minimum Drug Sentences: Throwing Away the Key or the Taxpayers' Money?" (MR-827-DPRC), Santa Monica, Calif.: RAND Corporation, 1997. © Copyright RAND 1997. All rights reserved.

Library of Congress Cataloging-in-Publication Data

Bardach, Eugene.
  A practical guide for policy analysis : the eightfold path to more effective problem solving / Eugene Bardach.— 2nd ed.
       p. cm.
  Includes bibliographical references and index.
  ISBN 1-56802-923-3 (alk. paper)
 1. Policy sciences. 2. Decision making. 3. Problem solving.   I. Title.

H97.B37 2005
320.6—dc22

2004020091

CONTENTS

PREFACE

This handbook serves as a guide to concepts and methods applied in the analysis of policy. I have developed the general approach and many of the specific suggestions over twenty-five years of teaching policy analysis workshops to first- and second-year graduate students at the Richard and Rhoda Goldman School of Public Policy, University of California, Berkeley. In the handbook's earliest incarnation, the ideas took form slowly and were conveyed to students in lectures. But because my faculty colleagues and I systematically overloaded our students with work, they would sometimes miss a lecture—and hence miss ideas that I regarded as essential. I determined that if I were to create a handout for the students, at least I would have discharged my responsibility, and it would be up to the students to retrieve the ideas they missed. Over the years, the hand-out grew, was disseminated informally to colleagues at other universities, and was posted on the Web site of the Electronic Hallway, based at the University of Washington. This book is the outgrowth of these previous compilations and the product of many years of experience.

The presumed user is a beginning practitioner preparing to undertake a policy analysis, such as one of our master's students at the Goldman School. But I have found this handbook useful at either end of the spectrum: in teaching undergraduate introduction to public policy courses as well as executive education groups.

The new edition of *A Practical Guide for Policy Analysis* is more user-friendly than the previous one. The book's organization has been streamlined so that core concepts and terms are easier to find, and the book's new design makes the presentation of the material simpler and more straightforward. More important, many users requested sample "real-world" policy documents that would more accurately reflect those discussed in the book. These readers should refer to the new Appendix A, where they will find the preface and summary of a policy brief by RAND researchers, chosen for its overall quality and clarity of presentation. I have annotated the brief to highlight the ways that this document is done "right."

The handbook assumes a familiarity with basic economic concepts, including those having to do with market failures (including market imperfections). It is not meant to stand alone but should be used in conjunction with other sources, including some of the best textbooks in policy analysis, which are cited often to amplify points in this handbook: Weimer and Vining 2004, Stokey and Zeckhauser 2004, Behn and Vaupel 1982, Friedman 2002, MacRae and Whittington 1997, and Morgan and Henrion 1990.

ACKNOWLEDGMENTS

I wish to acknowledge the patience and helpful response of the students and friends who have used this handbook, especially those who withstood its earlier versions. Special thanks are due Robert Behn, Sandford Borins, Jose Canela-Cacho, Hank Dempsey, David Dery, John Ellwood, Lee Friedman, David Garcia-Junco Machado, Nina Goldman, David Kirp, Jake Lavin, Leo Levenson, Martin A. Levin, Duncan MacRae, Sarah Marxer, Carolyn Marzke, John Mendeloff, Steven Page, Eric Patashnik, Beryl Radin, Andres Roemer, Larry Rosenthal, Mark Sabean, Eugene Smolensky, David Weimer, and Marc Zegans. I also thank Michael O'Hare, who has made very special contributions to this edition.

I wish to extend my thanks to my reviewers for their help with this edition: Matthew Cahn, California State University, Northridge, and Robert P. Goss, Brigham Young University. Thanks also go to Charisse Kiino, Elise Frasier, and Joan Gossett of CQ Press for their help in bringing this new edition to press. Many thanks to Katharine Miller as well for her sharp editorial recommendations.

Sasha Dobrovolsky deserves my gratitude more than anyone else, however. Sasha was in my undergraduate Public Policy 101 class in 1991.

An unusually gifted and entrepreneurial fellow, he once accosted me with this announcement: "Professor Bardach, these handouts you give us are outstanding. You should publish a book. When I graduate, I'm creating my own publishing house, and your book is the first I'm putting out." I said, "Sasha, you are surely mad. It's fine by me, but I am not going to be responsible for your financial losses. You are on your own." Alas, Sasha's publishing venture, Berkeley Academic Press, did not last long, but he went on to great success in other fields. I have unaccountably neglected to thank Sasha in the preface to earlier editions. I hope I am now making sufficient amends.

INTRODUCTION

Policy analysis is a social and political activity. True, you take personal moral and intellectual responsibility for the quality of your policy-analytic work. But policy analysis goes beyond personal decision making. First, the subject matter concerns the lives and well-being of large numbers of our fellow citizens. Second, the process and results of policy analysis usually involve other professionals and interested parties: it is often done in teams or officewide settings; the immediate consumer is a "client" of some sort, such as a hierarchical superior; and the ultimate audience will include diverse subgroups of politically attuned supporters and opponents of your work. All of these facts condition the nature of policy-analytic work and have a bearing on the nature of what is meant by "quality work."

A policy analyst can work in any number of positions. Once upon a time, the term implied someone rather wonkish who worked in a large government bureaucracy, serving up very technical projections of possible policy impacts for one or more policy alternatives to some undersecretary of planning. No longer. Policy analysts help in planning, budgeting, program evaluation, program design, program management, public relations, and other functions. They work alone, in teams, and in loose networks that cut across organizations. They work in the public, nonprofit, and for-profit spheres. Although their work is ideally distinguished by transparency of method and interpretation, the analysts themselves may explicitly bring to their jobs the values and passions of advocacy groups as well as "neutral" civil servants. The professional networks in which they work may contain—in most cases, do contain—professionals drawn from law, engineering, accounting, and so on, and in those settings the policy-analytic point of view has to struggle for the right to counter—or better yet, synthesize—the viewpoints of the other professionals. Although policy-analytic work products typically involve written reports, they may also include briefings, slide presentations, magazine articles, and television interviews. The recipients of these products may be broad and diffuse audiences as well as narrowly construed paying clients or employers. The advice in this handbook is directed both to policy analysts in practice and to students and others who, for whatever reasons, are attempting to look at the world through the eyes of a practitioner.

THE EIGHTFOLD PATH

Policy analysis is more art than science. It draws on intuition as much as method. Nevertheless, given the choice between advice that imposes too much structure on the problem-solving process and advice that offers too little, most beginning practitioners quite reasonably prefer too much. I have therefore developed the following approach, which I call the Eightfold Path:

- Define the Problem
- Assemble Some Evidence
- Construct the Alternatives
- Select the Criteria
- Project the Outcomes
- Confront the Trade-Offs
- Decide!
- Tell Your Story

These steps are not necessarily taken in precisely this order, nor are all of them necessarily significant in every problem. However, an effort to define the problem is usually the right starting place, and telling the story is almost inevitably the ending point. Constructing alternatives and selecting criteria for evaluating them must surely come toward the beginning of the process. Assembling some evidence is actually a step that recurs throughout the entire process, and it applies particularly to efforts to define the problem and to project the outcomes of the alternatives being considered.

The primary utility of this structured approach is that it reminds you of important tasks and choices that otherwise might slip your mind; its primary drawback is that, taken by itself, it can be mechanistic.

The Problem-Solving Process

The problem-solving process—being a process of trial and error—is iterative, so you usually must repeat each of these steps, sometimes more than once.

The spirit in which you take any one of these steps, especially in the earliest phases of your project, should be highly tentative. As you move through the problem-solving process, you will probably keep changing your problem definition, as well as your menu of alternatives, your set of evaluative criteria, and your sense of what evidence bears on the problem. With each successive iteration you will become a bit more confident that you are on the right track, that you are focusing on the right question, and so on. This can be a frustrating process, but it can also be rewarding—if you can learn to enjoy the challenges of search, discovery, and invention.

Some of the guidelines are practical, but most are conceptual.   Most of the concepts used will seem obvious, but there are exceptions. First, technical terms are sometimes employed. Second, some commonsense terms may be used in a special way that strips them of certain connotations and perhaps imports others. For the most part, all these concepts will become intelligible through experience and practice.

The concepts come embedded in concrete particulars.   In real life, policy problems appear as a confusing welter of details: personalities, interest groups, rhetorical demands, budget figures, legal rules and interpretations, bureaucratic routines, citizen attitudes, and so on. Yet the concepts described in this handbook are formulated in the abstract. You therefore need to learn to "see" the analytic concepts in the concrete manifestations of everyday life.

Caution: sometimes, some steps are already determined.   Suppose your client says, "We need an extra million dollars to run this program in the next budget year: find it." Does the Eightfold Path apply to this "analysis"? In a limited way. The client has already defined the problem and narrowed the relevant criteria very tightly. There won't be much creative scope for you when it comes to those steps. But all the other steps are likely to be relevant.

This challenge to "find it" is a simplified version of a more complex challenge—"Design it," as in "Figure out (that is, 'design') a way to protect this subway system from terrorist attack." Here, too, the problem definition step has already been settled by the client, though the other steps are likely to get the creative juices flowing. Ideas for dealing with design problems in general are given in the section on constructing alternatives (see p. 15).

Your Final Product

So what will your final product look like? Here is a very rough sketch of a typical written policy-analytic report: In a coherent narrative style you will describe some problem that needs to be mitigated or solved. You will lay out a few alternative courses of action that might be taken. To each course of action you will attach a set of projected outcomes that you think your client or audience would care about, suggesting the evidentiary grounds for your projections. If no alternative dominates all other alternatives with respect to all the evaluative criteria of interest, you will indicate the nature and magnitude of the trade-offs implicit in different policy choices. Depending on the client's expectations, you may state your own recommendation as to which alternative should be chosen.

The Spirit of the Eightfold Path

The spirit of the Eightfold Path is, I hope, an economizing and uplifting spirit. Analyzing public policy problems is a complex activity. It is easy to get lost, to waste a lot of time, to become demoralized. Other manuals and textbooks in policy analysis are very concerned that you get the analysis "right," in some sense. I hope this one will help in that respect, too. But, even more, I hope that this one will help you get it done with reasonable efficiency as well.

Finally, just as policy analysis originates in politics, so it concludes in politics. Political life has two sides to it: channeling conflict and building community. Policy analysis serves both sides. It channels conflict by showing that some arguments, and their proponents, are in some sense superior to others and deserve to win out. But it helps build community by marking off potential common ground as well. This is common ground defined by the rules and conventions of rational discourse—where opponents may employ analytical procedures to resolve disagreements, or where they may discover that at least some seemingly irreducible values conflicts can be recast as dry-as-dust technical disagreements over how much higher a probability Policy A has than Policy B for mitigating Problem P.

OVERVIEW OF THE BOOK

This is a book with many components. The primary component is Part I, describing the Eightfold Path and recommending heuristics to help you negotiate it.

Part II focuses on one particular step in the Eightfold Path: assembling evidence. It appeared thirty years ago as a journal article, but I have modified it for this edition and tried to integrate it better into the overall book in terms of both style and content. I include it because its objective is, I think, unique among the many prescriptive works in the social sciences and in journalism about data gathering and interpretation: it is above all concerned with using the researcher's time and energy efficiently.

Part III is also about a specialized topic in policy analysis not dealt with in other works: making use of ideas, and specimens of "smart practices," to be found in other sites. Imitation and adaptation are standard routes to progress (albeit occasionally, to regress) in other areas of life, so why not in public policy?

New in this edition is the first appendix, reflecting the preface and summary sections of a lengthy study by researchers at the RAND Corporation on the relative worth of mandatory minimum sentences for drug dealers. I introduce this material because many students and fellow teachers have told me it would be useful to provide a specimen of real, high-quality policy analysis, along with some commentary by myself. Institutionally, RAND is the oldest policy research organization in the country, if not the world. It has a deserved reputation for excellence. It also has a tradition of doing cost-effectiveness analysis, beginning with work for the military and, in the past two decades, branching into domestic policy. It is therefore particularly fitting to make use of a specimen produced by RAND.

Why this particular specimen? The reason is not that its conclusions are correct. I do not know enough about the drug policy field to have an opinion. I do know that these are highly respected researchers in the field and that the work selected here highlights the "Project the Outcomes" step in policy analysis, which I pronounce (see p. 35) "the hardest step," mostly because of the uncertainties involved in projecting the future. The chosen specimen wrestles in an interesting way with such uncertainties. It also makes a creative move in its approach to defining alternatives. And it illustrates clearly how to integrate strictly analytical work in a larger policy discussion rife with the value disagreements inevitably present in a democratic, pluralistic society.

The second appendix, "Things Governments Do," is a condensed survey of eleven types of governmental instruments for intervening in society and why one might or might not choose—if one has a choice—to make use of one rather than another. The third appendix is a summary of "semantic tips." It may not surprise readers to learn that semantic pitfalls abound on the Eightfold Path of policy analysis, but it will surely be more surprising that there are many semantic tricks to help policy analysis along. Tips about these appear throughout this entire volume, but I have collected them in Appendix C.

THE EIGHTFOLD PATH

The analytic work in problem-solving generally proceeds in a certain direction, from defining the problem at the beginning all the way to making a decision and explaining it at the end. But remember, this is a process much given to reconsidering, reviewing, changing one's mind—in other words, retracing one's steps on the path before starting out once more. Also, in some cases, the client or perhaps the political situation has already narrowed and focused the analytical task to such a degree that you need not even bother thinking through some of the steps. The exposition that follows lays out a generic process that must be adapted to a particular situation.

STEP ONE: DEFINE THE PROBLEM

Your first problem definition is a crucial step: it gives you both a reason for doing all the work necessary to complete the project and a sense of direction for your evidence-gathering activity. And in the last phases of the policy analysis, your final problem definition will probably help you structure how you *tell your story.*

Usually, the raw material for your initial problem definition comes from your client and derives from the ordinary language of debate and discussion in the client's political environment—language I call generically "issue rhetoric." This rhetoric may be narrowly confined to a seemingly technical problem or broadly located in a controversy of wide social interest. In either case, you have to get beneath the rhetoric to define a problem that is analytically manageable and that makes sense in light of the political and institutional means available for mitigating it.

Use the raw material of issue rhetoric with care. It often points to some condition of the world that people don't like or consider "bad" in some sense, such as "teenage pregnancy," "media violence," or "global warming." These evaluations do not necessarily need to be taken at face value. You will sometimes wish to explore the philosophical and empirical grounds on which you, your client, or others in your eventual audience should or should not consider the alleged condition "bad." Furthermore, issue rhetoric may point to some alleged—but not necessarily real— cause of the troubling condition, for example, "welfare" or "human wastefulness."

Issue rhetoric often has a partisan or ideological flavor. Although Americans cluster toward a mixed-ideology and pragmatic center, issue rhetoric is created by the more passionate and often more articulate individuals closer to the extremes. The great ideological divide in most developed democracies concerns the role of government assistance and regulation in solving problems relative to reliance on self, kin, and neighbors. Self-reliance is generally presumed to be the ideal, but this is a rebuttable presumption. "Liberal" issue rhetoric typically offers many rebuttals, usually involving distrust of "the market," but only some of these are grounded in realistic understanding of how markets do and do not work. "Conservative" issue rhetoric sometimes offers thoughtless defenses of "the market" but can also fall silent when favored business interests seek protectionist legislation. Because government as an institution is the chief alternative to private and community problem-solving, liberals and conservatives ideologize the question of just how competent and trustworthy it is. Selective perception abounds on both sides of this argument.

Generalities originating in issue rhetoric only sometimes suffice to settle concrete issues of policy choice and policy design, although economic theories of market failures and imperfections can often tell us when not to rely on the market, and Public Choice theories of government failure can often tell us when not to rely on the government (Weimer and Vining 2004; Glazer and Rotherberg 2001). As I explain later, policy analysis typically bridges all political ideologies by reliance on the normative standard of "maximizing welfare" and on social science theorizing about the comparative advantages of different institutions for different purposes. Thus you want not simply to echo the issue rhetoric in your problem definition, but to use it as raw material for a provisional problem definition that you hope will prove analytically useful.

Some issue labels may signify more than one problem. Depending on the audience, for example, "teenage pregnancy" may connote any or all of the following conditions: sexual immorality, the blighting of young people's and their children's life chances, exploitation of taxpayers, and social disintegration. Usually you will want to determine a primary problem focus, to ensure that the analysis does not get out of hand. But if the problems aren't too complicated, you may feel willing to define more than one.

Think of Deficit and Excess

It often—but not always—helps to think in terms of deficit and excess. For instance:

- "There are too many homeless people in the United States."
- "The demand for agricultural water is growing faster than our ability to supply it at an acceptable financial and environmental cost."
- "California's population of school-age children is growing at 140,000 per year, and our ability to develop the physical facilities in which to educate them is not growing nearly as fast."

It often helps to include the word *too* in the definition (e.g., "too big," "too small," "growing too slowly," "growing too fast"). These last two phrases (about "growing") remind us that problems deserving our attention don't necessarily exist "today" but are (at least potentially) in prospect for the future, whether near or distant.

However, it does not help to think in terms of deficit and excess when your problem is an already well-structured decision choice—for example, "Dump the dredging spoils either in the Bay or somewhere out in the Pacific Ocean." Nor does it help if your challenge is to invent *any* way to accomplish some defined objective—for example, "Find some grant funds to close the anticipated gap between revenues and expenditures." These decision- and invention-type challenges are problems *for* the policy analyst but are not the substantive sort of problems I am addressing in this section.

Make the Definition Evaluative

Remember that the idea of a "problem" usually means that people think there is something wrong with the world. But note that *wrong* is a very debatable term. Not everyone will think that the facts you (or others) have defined as a problem really do constitute a problem, for each person may apply a different evaluative framework to these facts. Unfortunately, there are no obvious or accepted ways to resolve philosophical differences of this type.

A common philosophical as well as practical question is "What private troubles warrant definition as public problems and thereby legitimately raise claims for amelioration by public resources?" It is usually helpful to view the situation through the "market failure" lens (Weimer and Vining 2004, chap. 5).[1] In its simplest formulation, market failure occurs when the technical properties of a good or service have one of the following effects:

- Making it hard to collect payment from all the potential beneficiaries—for instance, the large number of people who profit, albeit indirectly, from advances in basic science
- Making it hard to collect from the beneficiaries of consumption the true economic cost of making use of the good or service—such as the fresh air that vehicle owners use as a sink for their auto emissions
- Making it hard for consumers (and sometimes suppliers) to know the true qualities of the good or service they are acquiring—for instance, many repair-type services, including those performed by physicians as well as those performed by auto mechanics
- Making the cost of producing the marginal unit lower than the average cost within the relevant range of demand—such as a magazine article distributed via the Internet

It is impossible to overestimate the importance of this point, for in most—though not all—situations where no actual market failures can be

---

1. For a persuasive analysis of most traditional market failures in transaction cost terms, see Zerbe and McCurdy 1999, which also emphasizes the rich variety of interventions besides those undertaken by government to remedy traditionally conceived "market failures."

identified, people's private troubles *cannot* typically be ameliorated by even the most well-intentioned governmental interventions. And even when some amelioration is possible, there are usually many adverse side effects. In some cases, it may nevertheless be worthwhile to pay the price of these side effects, but such calculations must be done carefully and scrupulously.

Besides market failures, the main situations in which private troubles can warrant definition as public problems are these:

- Breakdowns of systems, such as family relationships, that occur largely outside markets
- Low living standards that arise precisely because markets do function well and do not reward individuals very generously if they lack marketable talents or skills
- The existence of discrimination against racial and other minorities
- The failure of government to function well in areas where it is traditionally expected to act effectively (e.g., in providing public schools)

Quantify If Possible

The definition should, insofar as possible, include a quantitative feature. Assertions of deficit or excess should come with *magnitudes* attached. How big is "too big"? How small is "too small"? How about "too slowly" or "too fast"? In terms of the examples cited earlier, how many homeless people are there in the United States? How many acre-feet of water are used now, and how does that amount compare with the demand in some specified future year (given certain assumptions about water pricing)? Exactly what is "our ability to develop physical facilities," and how do we expect it to grow, or shrink, over time?

If necessary, gather information to help you calibrate the relevant magnitudes. (See the discussion under "Assemble Some Evidence.")

In many or most cases, you will have to estimate—or, more likely, "guesstimate"—the magnitudes in question. Sometimes you should furnish a *range* as well as a *point* estimate of magnitudes—e.g., "Our best guess of the number of homeless persons in families is 250,000, although the truth could lie between 100,000 and 400,000."

Diagnose Conditions That Cause Problems

Some problematic conditions are not experienced as troublesome per se by citizens but are perceived by them, or by analysts working on their behalf, to be causes of trouble. It is sometimes useful to diagnose one or more alleged conditions of this type and to define them as problems to be mitigated or removed—as in, "One of the problems in the air pollution area is that states have not been willing to force motorists to keep their engines tuned up and their exhaust systems in proper order."

Note that this sort of problem definition is not merely descriptive but also diagnostic. It implicitly asserts that some condition, which may or may not be troubling to people per se, is an important cause of some other condition that is indeed troubling. Problem definitions that pretend to some diagnostic power can be useful, but they can also be treacherous. Suppose, after all, that the causal diagnosis is mistaken or misleading—for example, that states' unwillingness to enforce engine maintenance routines is *not* in fact a very important cause of air pollution. Because *definition* in some contexts connotes legitimate arbitrariness ("I'll define *justice* to mean . . .") the causal claims implicit in diagnostic problem definitions can easily escape needed scrutiny. (See "Project the Outcomes" for further discussion.)

Identify Latent Opportunities

A special kind of problem is an opportunity missed. Is it not rather small-minded to think of policy analysis as devoted merely to the amelioration of "problems"? May policy analysis not rise above the tedious and uninspiring business of patching and fixing? Can we not aspire to a world in which we can identify opportunities to do creative—not to say wonderful—things? "If it ain't broke, don't fix it" is a confining idea, and certainly policy analysts, policymakers, and public managers ought not to allow the "problem" focus to restrict the search for plausible opportunities. Unfortunately, the working agenda of most policy professionals is set by complaints, threats, worries, and troubles. There is often little time or energy left over to think about improvements that no one has identified as missing. Still, if latent opportunities are really lying around, it would be a pity to ignore them.

Where do we find opportunities for creative policy improvements that haven't first been identified by complaints, threats, and so on? Little academic or technical theory is available to answer this question. But Box I-1 contains a list that is suggestive.

Avoid Common Pitfalls in Problem Definition

Problem definition is a step beset by at least two dangerous pitfalls.

Defining the solution into the "problem."   Your problem definition should not include an implicit solution introduced by semantic carelessness. Projected solutions must be evaluated empirically and not legitimated merely by definition. Therefore, keep the problem definition stripped down to a mere description, and leave open where you will look for solutions.

- *Don't say:* "There is too little shelter for homeless families." Inadvertently implying that "more shelter" is the best solution may inhibit you from thinking about ways to prevent families from becoming homeless in the first place. *Try instead:* "Too many families are homeless."
- *Don't say:* "New schools are being built too slowly." Simply assuming that "more schools" is the solution could inhibit you from thinking about ways to use existing facilities more efficiently. *Try instead:* "There are too many schoolchildren relative to the currently available classroom space."

A tip-off that you're probably smuggling an implicit solution into the problem definition is to hear yourself saying, "Aha, but that's not the real problem; the real problem is . . ." While there are better and worse ways to conceptualize a problem, or to solve a problem, it stretches ordinary usage too much to say that one problem could be "more (or less) real" than another.

Accepting too easily the causal claims implicit in diagnostic problem definitions.   I suggested above that conditions that cause problems may also be problems. However, the causes must be real, not merely assumed. You have to evaluate the causal chain that goes from the situation itself to the

---

BOX I-1   **Some Generic Opportunities for Social Improvement That Often Go Unnoticed**

Operations research strategies.   By means of sequencing, timing, prioritizing, matching, clustering, and other such rationalizing arrangements, it is possible to use a fixed stock of resources to achieve higher productivity than would be possible otherwise. For instance, provided that traffic flow conditions are within certain parameters, high-occupancy-vehicle (HOV) lanes can maximize vehicle throughput in a fixed section of roadway.

Cost-based pricing.   Discrepancies between prices and real costs present an opportunity for enhancing social welfare by adjusting prices to better reflect the reality. For instance, introduce congestion tolls, or eliminate cross-subsidies for peak-period utilization of electricity, or remove rent controls.

By-products of personal aspirations.   It is possible to structure new incentives or create new opportunities for personal advantage or satisfaction that can indirectly result in social benefit—for example, offering to share the benefits of cost-reducing innovations with public-sector employees who conceive them and implement them.

Complementarity.   Two or more activities can potentially be joined so that each might make the other more productive—for example, public works construction and combating unemployment.

Input substitution.   The world abounds in opportunities to substitute less costly inputs in a current production process while achieving roughly equivalent results.

---

bad things it is alleged to cause, and to convince yourself that the causal relationship is real. For instance, for some people, "cocaine use" is not a problem in itself, but it might be a problem if it *leads to* crime, poor health, family disintegration, and so on. But does it lead to these outcomes, and to what degree? The evidence on this question should be evaluated very carefully before you decide it's okay to work with a problem definition involving "too much cocaine use."

Iterate

Problem definition is a crucial step. But because it is hard to get it right, you may take that same step again and again. Over the course of your

Development.   A sequence of activities or operations may be arranged to take advantage of a developmental process—for example, assessing welfare clients for employability and vocational interest before, rather than after, sending them out for job search.

Exchange.   There are unrealized possibilities for exchange that would increase social value. We typically design policies to simulate market-like arrangements—for example, pollution permit auctions, and arrangements to reimburse an agency for services it renders another agency's clients or customers.

Multiple functions.   A system can be designed so that one feature has the potential to perform two or more functions—for example, when a tax administrator dramatizes an enforcement case in such a way as both to deter potential violators and to reassure nonviolators that they are not being made into suckers for their honesty.

Nontraditional participants.   Line-level employees of public agencies often have knowledge of potential program improvements that could usefully be incorporated into the agencies' policies and operations. The same is true of the agencies' customers, clients, or the parties whom they regulate.

Underutilized capacity.   An example, in many communities, is school facilities that are utilized for relatively limited purposes for only part of the day and for only part of the year—although school officials would be quick to warn that tapping this capacity without harming school functions is not always easy.

analytic work, your empirical and conceptual understanding will evolve. For instance, you might start out thinking that the main problem is "too many halfway houses for the mentally ill in our city" but end up concluding that the main problem is how badly some of them are managed.[2] Also, as you begin to rule out alternative approaches to solving or mitigating your problem, you will probably want to sculpt the problem definition so that, in the end, you and the political system will have some

---

2. This happened to a graduate student group at the Goldman School whose client was the Oakland Police Department. They struggled hard to escape the initial assumptions held by their client and eventually to refocus their work.

chance of attacking the problem successfully. Finally, if you are working in an office or agency context, you will implicitly be negotiating a mutually acceptable problem definition with your analyst colleagues and your hierarchical superiors.[3]

STEP TWO: ASSEMBLE SOME EVIDENCE

All of your time doing a policy analysis is spent in two activities: thinking (sometimes aloud and sometimes with others) and hustling data that can be turned into evidence. Of these two activities, thinking is generally the more important, but hustling data takes much more time: reading documents, hunting in libraries, poring over studies and statistics, interviewing people, traveling to interviews, waiting for appointments, and so on.

The real-world settings in which policy analysis is done rarely afford the time for a research effort that would please a careful academic researcher. In fact, time pressure is probably almost as dangerous an enemy of high-quality policy analysis as politically motivated bias, if not more so. Therefore, it is essential to economize on your data collection activities. The key to economizing is this: try to collect only those data that can be turned into "information" that, in turn, can be converted into "evidence" that has some bearing on your problem.

For the logically minded, here are some definitions: *Data* are facts —or, some might say, representations of facts—about the world. Data include all sorts of statistics but go well beyond statistics, too. Data also include, for instance, facts about an agency manager's ability to deal constructively with the press. *Information* is data that has "meaning," in the sense that it can help you sort the world into different logical or empirical categories. The prevalence of cigarette smoking in five different coun-

---

3. Some analysts also claim that it is simply not worthwhile to define as "problems" conditions that cannot be ameliorated: "Problems are better treated as opportunities for improvement; defined problems, as problems of choice between alternative means to realize a given opportunity. The process of problem definition would then be one of search, creation, and initial examination of ideas for solution until a problem of choice is reached." See Dery 1984, 27.

tries is data, but these data become information when you decide it is interesting to array the countries comparatively (e.g., from lowest to highest prevalence). *Evidence* is information that affects the existing beliefs of important people (including yourself) about significant features of the problem you are studying and how it might be solved or mitigated. Differential prevalence of smoking, for instance, can become evidence bearing on hypotheses concerning differential levels of concern about personal health across countries.

You need evidence for three principal purposes, all of which are relevant to the goal of producing realistic projections of possible policy outcomes. One purpose is to assess the nature and extent of the problem(s) you are trying to define. A second is to assess the particular features of the concrete policy situation you are engaged in studying. For instance, you may need to know—or guess—about agency workloads, recent budget figures, demographic changes in a service area, the political ideology of the agency chief, the competency of the middle-level managers in the agency, and the current attitudes of some other agency that nominally cooperates with this one on some problem. The third purpose is to assess policies that have been thought, by at least some people, to have worked effectively in situations apparently similar to your own, in other jurisdictions, perhaps, or at other times. (Sometimes these situations will have been evaluated statistically and sometimes not: see Part III, " 'Smart (Best) Practices' Research: Understanding and Making Use of What Look Like Good Ideas from Somewhere Else.")

Because each of these purposes becomes salient in different phases of the policy analysis process, this "Assemble Some Evidence" step on the Eightfold Path will be taken more than once, but with a different focus each time.

Think Before You Collect

Thinking and collecting data are complementary activities: you can be a much more efficient collector of data if you think, and keep on thinking, about what you do and don't need (or want) to know, and why. The principal—and exceedingly common—mistake made by beginners and veterans alike is to spend time collecting data that have little or no potential to be developed into evidence concerning anything you actually care about. People often do this because running around collecting data looks and feels productive, whereas first-rate thinking is hard and frustrating. Also, when they see you busily collecting data, the people paying for your work tend to be reassured that somehow they are getting their money's worth.

The value of evidence.   Since most evidence is costly to produce, you must weigh its likely cost against its likely value. How is its likely value to be estimated? The answer may be cast in a decision-analytic framework (decision trees), though you should remember that the process of making a decision involves a great many elements prior to the moment of actual choice, such as defining a useful problem, thinking up better candidate solutions, and selecting a useful model. In general, the value of any piece of evidence depends on these factors:

- The likelihood that it will cause you to substitute some better decision for whatever decision you would have made without it (which might have been an "acceptable" decision in and of itself)
- The likelihood that the substituted decision will, directly or indirectly, produce a better policy outcome than the outcome that would have been produced by the original decision
- The magnitude of the difference in value between the likely-to-be improved outcome and the original outcome

The utility of an educated guess.   It is surprising how well you can do in many cases by gathering no evidence at all but simply sitting down and thinking something through and then making some serious educated guesses. There is nothing shameful about acting on such guesstimates and thereby conserving your data-collecting time and energies for answering questions for which good evidence is really necessary (see Part II, "Assembling Evidence").

A helpful check on yourself, to avoid collecting useless data, is to ask yourself the following questions before embarking on some data collection venture:

- "Suppose the data turn out to look like so-and-so as opposed to thus-and-such. What implication would that have for my understanding of how to solve this problem?"

- "Compared to my best guess about how the data will look once I've got them, how different might they look if I actually took the trouble to get them?"
- "How much is it worth to me to confirm the actual difference between what I can guess and what I can learn about the world by really getting the data?"

It is this sort of critical attitude about the value of expensive data collection that often leads good and experienced policy analysts to make do with back-of-the-envelope estimates. However, none of the above is meant to be an excuse for shirking the job of getting good data—and sometimes lots of them, at huge costs in time and money—when you've convinced yourself that the investment really would pay off. There's an obvious and critical difference between justifiable and unjustifiable guesstimates.

Review the Available Literature

There is hardly a problem without some academic discipline or professional association doing research on its causes and solutions. It is easy to find journals and various professional publications disseminating research results, theories, case studies, the musings of experienced practitioners, and so on. The Internet brings much of this to your desktop, but some of the best vehicles are better accessed by browsing the periodical shelves of university or government libraries.

Advocacy organizations often publish a great deal of interesting work and may take special pains to disseminate their work on the Internet. However, there is a danger of relying too much on such sources just because they are readily available.

Survey "Best Practices"

The chances are that the problem you are studying is not unique, and that policymakers and public managers in other jurisdictions, perhaps not very different from the one you are studying, have dealt with it in some fashion. See if you can track down some of these past solutions and extrapolate them to the situation you are studying. The extrapolation process is complicated, though (see Part III, " 'Smart (Best) Practices' Research").

Use Analogies

Sometimes it pays to gather data about things that are, on the surface, quite unlike the problem you are studying but that, on a deeper level, show instructive similarities. For instance, your understanding of how a merit pay plan for compensating managers in the public sector might work could perhaps be improved by seeing how similar schemes work in the private sector. Or, if you are working on the problem of how a state can discipline, and perhaps disbar, incompetent attorneys, you might usefully spend a good deal of your time learning about how the medical profession handles problems of physician incompetence. If you are working on how to reduce neighborhoods' resistance to accepting low-income housing projects, you could usefully look into the literature on community resistance to accepting solid-waste incinerators.

As these examples suggest, some analogies are easier to perceive, and to make sense of, than others. It takes a little imagination to see instructive analogies and, occasionally, a little daring to try to convince others to see both the usefulness of the analogy and its inevitable limitations.

Start Early

You are often dependent on the busy schedules of other very busy people whom you ask to furnish you with information or opportunities for interviews. It is extremely important to submit requests for information—and especially for interviews—well in advance of when you want to have completed the data collection. (For a useful description of how to conduct literature reviews, library searches, phone interviews, and personal interviews, see Weimer and Vining 2004, chap. 13; see also Part II, "Assembling Evidence.")

Touch Base, Gain Credibility, Broker Consensus

The process of assembling evidence inevitably has a political as well as a purely analytical purpose. Sometimes it entails touching base with potential critics of your work so they will not be able to complain later that you have ignored their perspectives. By making yourself known to potential supporters of your work, you may also be able to create a cadre of defenders.

A more complex objective, where appropriate, might be to blend policy analysis with the process of improving a policy idea or decision during the course of implementation. (See the following discussion of "improvability" as a criterion.) This objective entails obtaining "feedback" from participants, usually in an iterative process, and sharing some of your own reactions with them. You thereby become more of a partner in the process than an outside observer and diagnostician. An even more complex and challenging role is for you to become a particular type of "partner," a facilitator and broker, whether by acting as a conduit from one person to another or by convening meetings and other gatherings.

Free the Captive Mind

In exchange for access to data and a ready-made worldview, researchers sometimes uncritically accept problem definitions and preferred solutions from kindly informants (not to mention from paying clients or employers). To counter such temptations, be sure to make contact with individuals or factions whom you would expect to disagree—the more sharply the better—with your kindly informants. A time-saving, but only partial, substitute is to ask your kindly informant, "Who might object strongly to your point of view about this, and why might they do so?"

STEP THREE: CONSTRUCT THE ALTERNATIVES

By *alternatives* I mean something like "policy options," or "alternative courses of action," or "alternative strategies of intervention to solve or mitigate the problem."

Start Comprehensive, End Up Focused

In the last stages of your analysis, you won't want to be assessing more than three or four principal alternatives, but in the beginning, you should err on the side of comprehensiveness. Make a list of all the alternatives you might wish to consider in the course of your analysis. Later on you will discard some obvious losers, combine others, and reorganize still others into a single "basic" alternative with one or more subsidiary "variants." For your initial list, though, where should you turn for ideas?

One starting point would be to note the alternatives that key political actors are actively proposing or seem to have on their minds. These may include people's pet ideas, institutions' inventories of "off-the-shelf" proposals that simply await a window of opportunity, and prepackaged proposals that political ideologues are perennially advocating. Then you could try to *invent* alternatives that might prove to be superior to the alternatives currently being discussed by the key political actors. It's good to brainstorm, to try to be creative—but don't expect that you will necessarily produce much better ideas than those other people have already advanced.

One way to coax your creativity is to refer to the checklist in Appendix B, "Things Governments Do." For each entry on the list, ask yourself, "Might it make sense to try some version of this generic strategy to help mitigate this problem?" Because it is a comprehensive list, the answer with respect to any single strategy will usually be negative. Going through the list systematically is worthwhile, however. Because the list is not very long, with experience you will need to spend only a few minutes to decide whether any ideas there might be worth considering further. (See also the very valuable discussion on generic policy instruments in Weimer and Vining 2004, chap. 10.)

Always include in your first approach to the problem the alternative "Let present trends continue undisturbed." You need to do this because the world is full of naturally occurring change, and some of these ongoing changes may mitigate the problem on which you are working. (Note that I am not characterizing this alternative as "Do Nothing." It is not possible to "do nothing" or to "not decide." Most of the trends in motion will probably persist and alter the problem, whether for better or for worse.)

To see if "natural" change will affect the scope of the problem, inspect its most common sources in the public policy environment: (1) political changes following elections, as well as changes induced by the prospect of having to contest an election; (2) changes in unemployment and inflation rates that accompany the business cycle; (3) the changing "tightness" or "looseness" of agency budgets caused by overall taxing and spending policies; and (4) demographic changes, such as population migration patterns and population "bulges" moving through certain ages. In most cases, however, this "let-present-trends-continue" option will drop out of your final analysis. It follows that if you do your problem definition work well, you will end up with an important problem in your sights that in most cases can be mitigated to some degree by some affirmative action.

Model the System in Which the Problem Is Located

We often think about alternative approaches to the problem as possible *interventions* in the system that holds the problem in place or keeps it going. Logically, it is not necessary to model the causes of a problem in order to cure it—pharmaceutical manufacturers can testify that many of their successful products work by unknown causal routes on conditions whose causes are not at all understood. But a good causal model is often quite useful for suggesting possible "intervention points." This is especially true when the problem is embedded in a complex system of interacting forces, incentives, and constraints—which is usually the case. Consider, for instance, a system that produces "too much traffic congestion" at some choke point such as a bridge or a tunnel. A sketch of the relevant causal model would include the demand for travel along the relevant route, the available modes of travel, the amount of roadway capacity, and the price to users of roadway capacity. An efficient and simple—but usually politically unpopular—intervention might be to increase the price to users so as to reflect the degree to which each user contributes to congestion and increased travel times.

How self-conscious, elaborate, and rigorous should your causal model be? Many social scientists who devote themselves to policy analysis would hold, "The more so the better." I say, "Yes, but . . ." Self-consciousness is highly desirable. Elaborateness (or comprehensiveness, in this case a near synonym) is desirable because it decreases the risk of missing important causal connections, but it can blur the analytic focus and blunt creativity in designing intervention strategies. Rigor is desirable if it prevents you from relying on unarticulated and false assumptions; its downside is that you might exclude factors that are important—for instance, the personalities of certain actors—because you don't know how to model their effect rigorously and/or because you have only hunches regarding the nature of the relevant personalities.

Many models are best thought of as elaborations of a fundamental metaphor. They can be mathematically precise or verbal and evocative. Some commonly used metaphors that are the bases for models of particular value in designing alternatives are discussed in the following sections.

Market models.   Note that the model of a market where disaggregated suppliers exchange goods or services with disaggregated demanders can apply to unpriced goods and services. The main idea behind the market model is really equilibration through exchange. Hence, the market model can be applied to many phenomena other than the production and allocation of textbook goods such as widgets or apples.

For instance, you might try to understand the flow of patients into a state mental hospital system in terms of supply and demand: there is a fixed short-run "supply" of available beds in state hospitals and a per diem charge for each, and a complex "demand" for their use generated by police departments, county psychiatric emergency units, judges, members of the public, and so on.

A standard intervention strategy for improving markets that are not working as well as they might is to find some way to raise or lower the prices faced by either suppliers or demanders.

Production models.   Unfortunately, there is not much academic literature about the operating logics of the common types of production systems found in public policy—e.g., command-and-control regulation, the provision of information, and all the other "Things Governments Do" briefly described in Appendix B. (However, see Weimer and Vining 2004, chap. 10, on "generic policies"; Salamon 2002.) In any case, the main concern in understanding production systems should be to identify the parameters whose values, when they move out of a certain range, make the systems most vulnerable to breakdown, fraud and abuse, egregious diseconomies, and the distortion of intended purpose. It is also helpful to know about those parameters that matter most when we try to upgrade a production system from mere adequacy to performance levels we might think of as "excellent" (see Part III, on " 'Smart (Best) Practices' Research").

Another way to look at production models is through optimization lenses. Operations research models—e.g., queuing, inventory management, Markov processes—are relevant here. (For a good, brief discussion, see Stokey and Zeckhauser 1978; and Victorio 1995; also see the models, particularly that of case management, in Rosenthal 1982.)

Evolutionary models.   An evolutionary model describes a common process of change over time. It is constructed of three important subprocesses: variation among competitors, selection, and retention. Suppose, for instance, that in an agency enforcing health-related standards in the workplace, the complaints disproportionately concerned visible and annoying problems that were not, however, as hazardous to worker health as less visible and annoying problems. In this case, the evolutionary model suggests several plausible intervention points. The agency might try to educate workers to detect and complain about more serious problems, contriving thereby to swamp the less serious problems—thus changing the pool of "competitors." It might start screening the complaints for their likelihood of being associated with more fruitful targets—thus changing the "selection mechanism." Or it might attempt to persuade workers, and perhaps their union representatives, to reduce their propensity to complain about matters the agency wishes to hear less about—thus changing the "retention mechanism," workers' attitudes. (For other ideas and an excellent discussion of the uses of models generally, see Lave and March 1975.)

Conceptualize and Simplify the List of Alternatives

The final list of alternatives—the one you include in your presentation to your client and other audiences—will almost certainly look quite different from the one you started with. Not only will you have thrown some out that just don't look very good, but you will also have done some work to *conceptualize* and *simplify* alternatives.

The key to conceptualization is to try to sum up the basic strategic thrust of an alternative in a simple sentence or even a phrase. This is difficult but usually worth the effort. It usually helps to use very plain, short phrases stripped of jargon. When the Environmental Protection Agency (EPA) was created, the first administrator confronted (a partial list of) alternatives that might have been described thus: "Let the states do the work; let the feds give them the money"; "Remove impediments to firms cooperating on antipollution research"; and "Sue the bastards" (meaning the large, visible polluting firms and industries, the prosecution of which would help build political support for the new agency).

The key to simplification is to distinguish between a basic alternative and its variants. The basic element in many policy alternatives is an intervention strategy, such as regulatory enforcement or a subsidy or a tax incentive, that causes people or institutions to change their conduct in some way.[4] But no intervention strategy can stand alone; it must be implemented by some agency or constellation of agencies (perhaps including nonprofit organizations), and it must have a source of financing. Usually the variants on the basic strategy are defined by different methods of implementation and different methods of financing.

The distinction between a basic strategy and variants based on implementation details is especially helpful when you have a lot of possible solutions to consider and you need to reduce the complexity involved in comparing them. Making the distinction puts you in a position to break your analysis into successive steps. In the first step you might compare three "basic" alternatives, say, while ignoring the details described by their "variants." Then, once you have decided on one of these "basic" alternatives, you would turn to comparing the variants.

For example: You want to decrease the prevalence of heroin use in your county by 50 percent over the next five years.[5] You consider three basic alternatives: methadone maintenance, law enforcement pressure, and drug education. Potential variants for each one have to do with the funding sources, in that state, federal, and county money can be used in different degrees (although not all mixes of funds available for one approach are also available for the other two). Variation is also possible according to who administers the program(s): nonprofit organizations, county employees, or state employees. Or, you might consider vari-

---

4. Often, though not always, the basic element is something like a smart practice— that is, an intervention strategy that attempts to take advantage of some qualitative opportunity to create valued change at relatively low cost and/or risk. See Part III, " 'Smart (Best) Practices' Research."
5. Choosing a numerical target can help focus energies and can force you to think about what effects are too small to be worth doing. But when all increments are of equal value, choosing a target may be arbitrary and self-defeating.

ants of scale and scope, such as two possible sizes for your methadone program.

Design Policy Alternatives

This handbook assumes throughout that you are working on a problem of policy choice. However, a special case of policy choice occurs when you wish to, or have to, *design* at least one policy alternative to put into the menu of possibilities. Maybe you are just not satisfied with the menu of alternatives that people in the policy environment are already talking about.

Looking around.   Perhaps the problem you are dealing with is so new or unique that you will be the first, or even the only, person to oversee the needed design work. More likely, though, others have dealt with this problem already. It pays to see what they have done and to assess the degree of success or failure. Successful approaches are usually the most helpful, but sometimes you can learn a lot from evident failures as well.

Where to look? It may help to observe sister jurisdictions or institutions. If you are thinking about a problem at the state level, look to other states; at the city level, to other cities; at the community foundation level, to other community foundations. Professional associations linking government officials (such as chief state school officers, district attorneys, county welfare directors, etc.) often publish materials describing "best practice" in one or more of their member jurisdictions; even if they do not, a phone call to the executive offices of the association may produce useful leads. However, it may be necessary to consider whether the problems in your "target" jurisdiction and the "source" jurisdiction are similar in nature and scale. A city that has nearly solved its homeless problem with a service-rich mix of supportive housing and solicitous outreach (e.g., Philadelphia) may or may not be a source of good ideas for a city with a problem that is four or five times as large per capita and a physical climate that is very mild and therefore attractive (e.g., San Francisco). You may discover that although the source's ideas are very good indeed, they will need to be adapted to the target jurisdiction's particular context. (For more on how to deal with this "extrapolation problem," see Part III, on " 'Smart (Best) Practices' Research.")

Design problems are generally of two types. One involves the management of "cases," by which I mean individuals or other entities, such as firms or communities or lower levels of government, that receive some kind of "treatment." The treatment might be delivery of a subsidy, imposition of obligations, or application of some sort of person-changing regime (such as educating children or getting offenders to "go straight"). The second principal type of design problem involves operating on a collectivity of some kind rather than on individual cases—for example, improving traffic flow, eliminating corruption in the police department, preserving habitat, or launching a community cleanup campaign. The second type is too varied to discuss here, but a program that manages cases fits a rough template. That is, we can lay out a general procedure and list questions that should be asked.

Managing cases. I use the term *program* deliberately, to refer to an organized ensemble of routines. For instance, a program to distribute subsidies has routines for determining eligibility, calculating the amount to be paid, and detecting and deterring fraud and abuse. A regulatory program has routines for enforcing compliance with its rules, including inspection procedures and formulas for applying sanctions. It might also have routines for adopting rules, giving technical assistance to regulated parties, and offering forbearance in exchange for more efforts to cooperate. In a person-changing program, the routines typically bring the subjects into a setting where change is to be rewarded, facilitated, induced, or demanded, and where professionals apply a whole kit of tools to the change process. Think of schoolchildren, classrooms, and teachers; or of patients, hospitals, and doctors; or of welfare recipients, training programs, and caseworkers and trainers.

Such routines operate at the level of the individual case—sometimes called the "street level." Design problems at this level usually are mild compared to those that emerge at the level of the aggregate of cases, the population level. At the street level, we normally apply performance criteria of effectiveness, efficiency, fairness, and helpfulness. At the population level, we discover that design trade-offs must normally be made between all these criteria. These trade-offs occur primarily because (1) agencies never seem to have enough resources to treat all cases as we would ideally like them to be treated, and (2) standard operating procedures of the sort that government employs in the name of consistency and non-arbitrariness can bend only so far in trying to cope with the diversity and heterogeneity of the real world.

In confronting the inevitable design trade-offs, it helps to look at any set of routines from two perspectives: that of the case manager in the agency and that of the citizen whose case is being "treated." It often happens that routines designed to make life easier for program staff only make life harder for citizens. ("Sorry, we don't give advice about that; send in the application and we'll respond . . .")

It also helps to remember occasionally to go back to basics, to reiterate to yourself and others the main objective of the program. What social problem is supposed to be ameliorated? Or what existing program is to be redesigned to accomplish what objective better? Doing so presents an opportunity to think also about an often-neglected but very important design issue of a more instrumental kind: what evidence will you systematically collect in the course of normal program operations that can let program managers know whether they are succeeding? That is, what tracking and evaluation routines can be designed and put in place?

Making arguments "for the sake of discussion. . . ."   Consider what is involved in designing a house, an office building, a living room, a dance production, a theater set, a fund-raising event, a political campaign, a graduate public policy curriculum, a nonprofit environmental education organization that will operate on a national scale, or a profit-seeking organization that will manufacture and market cyberwidgets in ten to twenty national markets. Clearly, design is a complex process, requiring many iterations, in which you both explore different ways to accomplish a certain set of objectives and alter the set of objectives in light of what you learn about what is actually practicable.

In some cases, the policy analyst works on the design problem more or less alone, like some brooding master architect. More likely, she does her work in loose or tight conjunction with other policy professionals who bring different sorts of expertise (e.g., legal, engineering, fiscal) to the table, and who bring different viewpoints and priorities as well. In any case, sooner or later, the design work will be held out for much more public view. Interested stakeholders, and perhaps more diverse audiences, who have previously been unaware of the design work going on seemingly behind the scenes, will see what you're up to. And they will offer their reactions.

You will want to use such reactions for two purposes: to improve your design according to criteria that you and your client—and very likely your audiences—think are important, including the criterion of political feasibility; and to respond in such a way as to increase the political support (and decrease the opposition) that may come your way, now or later, on process grounds alone. I shall not discuss here the strategy and tactics involved in how to communicate with different audiences or the sequence in which to do so. I limit discussion to the questions of just how rough or polished the design should be that you first subject to relatively public review and comment and how tentatively you should put it forward.

Not surprisingly, a middle ground is best. A very rough and admittedly tentative design may leave out important points, creating a sort of vacuum that outside interests will rush to fill on their own terms. You will then be forced onto the defensive, as you try to forestall the solution they have been first to suggest. Moreover, a very rough design may signal that the design work is at such a preliminary stage that it is not worth the trouble (or the risk of early-mover vulnerability) for any of the stakeholders to react at all. On the other hand, an overly polished and seemingly definitive design may signal stakeholders that you are not interested in consulting them. In that case, they may feel that they have no choice but to oppose your design more vehemently than they otherwise might have done—unless, of course, they conclude that they have no choice but to get onboard and negotiate for the best terms they can manage.

Assuming you put out a rough-but-not-too-rough design and elicit a range of fairly thoughtful opinion as a result, you will need ways to keep in touch with the variety of actors who now expect—and whom you may wish—to be part of an ongoing, if rather diffuse, design process. Keeping in touch will require a communications infrastructure (telephone, fax machine, e-mail), of course. It will also require efforts on your part to develop the sort of network relationships that permit rapid and reasonably trustworthy interpersonal communications.

THE EIGHTFOLD PATH   25

At a more analytical level—because any design must be anchored in working assumptions about its objectives, available resources, and constraints—you should choose your assumptions with an eye to their reasonableness as "a basis for further discussion." You may feel some discomfort at putting forward such assumptions because they are hypothetical or speculative, and because critics might therefore challenge them as "lacking in rigor." Policy analysis is not only an exercise in truth-telling, however, but a pragmatic and responsible effort to facilitate reasonable discourse about a policy future that is inherently uncertain.

Beware a Linguistic Pitfall

Alternative does not necessarily signify that the policy options are mutually exclusive. Policy analysts use the term ambiguously: sometimes it means one choice that implies foregoing another, and sometimes it means simply one more policy action that might help solve or mitigate a problem, perhaps in conjunction with other alternatives. You should be aware of the ambiguity in other people's usage, and in telling your story (Step Eight) you should be sure that no such ambiguity enters your own usage.

Sometimes you won't be entirely sure whether two alternatives are or are not mutually exclusive. For instance, although the mayor may have promised enough money to either fix potholes or provide homeless shelters (but not both), you may have made such a great case for both programs that the mayor may decide to increase the budgetary allocation.

STEP FOUR: SELECT THE CRITERIA

It helps to think of any policy story (see Step Eight) as having two interconnected but separable plot lines, the analytical and the evaluative. The first is all about facts and disinterested projections of consequences, while the second is all about value judgments. Ideally, all analytically sophisticated and open-minded persons can agree, more or less, on the rights and wrongs in the analytical plot and on the nature of its residual uncertainties. But this is not true with regard to the evaluative plot—where we expect subjectivity and social philosophy to cavort more freely. The analytical plot will reason about whether X, Y, or Z is likely to happen, but it is in the evaluative plot that we learn whether we think X or Y or Z is good or bad for the world.

This fourth step in the Eightfold Path belongs primarily to the evaluative plot line. It is the most important step for introducing values and philosophy into the policy analysis, because some possible "criteria" are evaluative standards used to judge the goodness of the projected policy outcomes associated with each of the alternatives.

Of course, the most important evaluative criterion is that the projected outcome will solve the policy problem to an acceptable degree. But this is only the beginning. After all, any course of action is likely to affect the world in many ways, some desired and some not. Each of those effects—or projected outcomes, to return to our Eightfold Path language—requires a judgment on our part as to whether and why it is thought desirable. Our set of criteria embodies such judgments. Because any significant impact cries out for such a judgment to be made, the greater the variety of significant impacts, the richer will be the set of evaluative criteria we will need to deal with them.

Please note that evaluative criteria are *not* used to judge the alternatives, or at least not directly. They are to be applied to the projected outcomes. It is easy to get confused about this point—and to get the analysis very tangled as a result. This confusion is encouraged by a common-sense way of speaking: "Alternative A looks to be the best; therefore let's proceed with it." But this phrasing ignores a very important step: the complete formulation is "Alternative A will very probably lead to Outcome O_A, which we judge to be the best of the possible outcomes; therefore, we judge Alternative A to be the best." Applying criteria to the evaluation of outcomes and not of alternatives makes it possible to remember that we might like O_A a great deal even if, because we lack sufficient confidence that A would actually lead to O_A, we decide not to choose Alternative A after all. With that judgment on the table, it would be possible to look for other alternatives with a greater likelihood of producing O_A.

Commonly Used Evaluative Criteria

Efficiency.   Typically, the efficiency criterion is the most important evaluative consideration in cost-effectiveness and cost-benefit studies. I use *efficiency* more or less as the term is used in economics, for maximizing the aggregate of individuals' welfare as that welfare would be construed by the individuals themselves—in economic jargon, "Maximize the sum of individual utilities," or "Maximize net benefits." Another roughly equivalent formulation would be "Maximize the public interest."

Note that although *efficiency* has an antiseptic, technocratic, and elitist ring to it, the insistence here that "utilities" are to be assessed according to individual citizens' construction of their own welfare is thoroughly democratic. Indeed, siding with efficiency—on average, across most policy issues and policy decisions—is a way to produce more humanistic policy results, too. The reason is not that efficiency is so very humane, but that policy decisions failing to consider efficiency very often fail to take account of the welfare of the little guy at all. The little guy may be little, but in a proper efficiency analysis, he at least shows up to be counted. Efficiency analysis imposes a moral check (for whatever that is worth in the real world of politics) on political visionaries eager to relocate entire populations so as to make room for dams, and on special interests eager to impose seemingly small price increases on large numbers of consumers through protectionist measures in order to maintain the incomes of a relatively small number of producers.

We should observe, though, that from the point of view of social justice, the efficiency criterion may be somewhat limited. First, because analysts typically estimate people's "utility" by inferring their willingness to pay for some benefit (or to be spared some deprivation), individuals with less money do not, in an analytical sense, have as much clout as those with more. Just how big a limitation this analytical antiegalitarianism turns out to be will depend on particular cases, however. Second, if the values at stake have few or no human defenders, and therefore no human pocketbooks to back an estimate of willingness to pay, the efficiency criterion might underestimate these values even if by some conception of justice they ought to be weighted heavily. In theory, ecological values are the main example, although in fact some ecological values do have human defenders who derive enormous utility from preserving them—a utility that would be accounted for in a proper efficiency analysis.

Although cost-effectiveness (CE) analysis and benefit-cost (BC) analysis sound alike and are frequent traveling companions, they are not the same, and their uses can be quite different. True, both conceptualize a domain of benefits accruing to individual citizens valued in terms of their utility. And both construe the policy problem as involving some production relationship between resources and welfare-increasing outcomes. However, CE takes one or the other of these (either resources or outcomes) as fixed or targeted; the analysis then tries to find the best means to manipulate the other one (either maximizing the benefits, given the level of assumed resources, or minimizing the amount of resources, given the targeted outcome requirement). BC, on the other hand, allows both resources and outcomes to be treated as variable in scale. It is therefore more complicated than CE, for while both BC and CE concern themselves with the productive efficiency of the program or project, BC is additionally concerned with the program's scale.

CE analysis is much more common than BC analysis. Indeed, a surprisingly large number of policy issues can be simplified and stylized as CE problems, even though on the surface they may not appear to be likely candidates at all for this sort of treatment. Here are two examples:

- The Mudville mayor wishes to respond to business complaints that building permits "take forever" to obtain. Given that you can spend no more than $500 and are permitted to change the work flow in the city planning office but not personnel assignments, the CE framework might suggest minimizing delay arising from purely procedural and bureaucratic sources.
- Quake City must upgrade the seismic safety of several thousand buildings constructed of unreinforced masonry. You have a twenty-year time span and no immediate budget constraint, but you wish to accomplish the job with minimum disruption to the lives (and incomes) of the residents and small businesses that may be temporarily displaced by the building renovation process. In order to minimize such disruption, CE analysis might lead you to propose that the work be done in one season rather than another, or that not all grocery stores be closed at once, or that tenants be assisted in organizing mutual aid groups.

Equality, equity, fairness, "justice."   There are, of course, a great many different, and often opposed, ideas about what these terms do, or should, mean. Not only ought you yourself to think hard about these ideas, but sometimes you should also take your audience through some of that thinking, as in the following examples:

- In California, drivers who do not carry liability insurance leave persons whom they injure in auto accidents at risk of being under-compensated. Many of those who "go bare" are relatively poor. Many other drivers purchase their own insurance against exactly this risk ("uninsured-motorist coverage"). A policy proposal to pay for all drivers' liability insurance out of a fund created by sur-charges at the fuel pump was denounced by some observers as "inequitable" to the poor, who currently go bare of insurance. Other observers said that those who go bare impose inequitable premium expenses or risks of undercompensation on the rest of society, including many individuals who are themselves poor or not very well off. Clearly the analyst needs to include a discussion of the idea of equity.
- The current debate over whether to retain affirmative action pref-erences for African Americans and certain other minorities in uni-versity admissions is sometimes said to pit fairness to individuals against justice to social groups. This is odd, though, since some philosophers—and most ordinary folk, too—suppose that no sys-tem claiming to be just could contain any features deemed unfair. Again, the analyst has a job to do in sorting out ideas and language.

Freedom, community, and other ideas. To stimulate thought, here is a (far from complete) list with more ideas about evaluative criteria of pos-sible relevance: free markets, economic freedom, capitalism, "freedom from government control," equality before the law, equality of opportu-nity, equality of result, free speech, religious freedom, privacy, safety (especially from chemicals, various environmental hazards, etc.), neigh-borliness, community, sense of belonging, order, security, absence of fear, traditional family structure, egalitarian family structure, empowerment of workers, maintenance of a viable nonprofit sector, voluntarism, trust in others.

Process values. American democracy values process and procedure (e.g., having a say in policy issues that affect you, rationality, openness and accessibility, transparency, fairness, non-arbitrariness) as well as substance. These considerations probably apply to the very design or decision process for which you are doing your present analytic work. Therefore remember to consult broadly and equitably. In addition to building up legitimacy for your work, you may be surprised at how much you can learn, especially from people who are very unlike yourself socially or ideologically. This does not, of course, mean that you should in the end give equal deference to all opinions or desires, or keep the consultative process open forever. Some opinions are more creditable than others, and at some point consultation must give way to decision.

Weighting Conflicting Evaluative Criteria

As we saw in the case of defining the problem, when values are at issue, as they are in regard to criterion selection as well, we must reckon how to weight opposing values. There are two general approaches to this problem.

The political process takes care of it.   One approach is simply to allow existing governmental and political processes to determine the weighting. Typically, this approach will accord primacy to the analyst's employer or client, with derivative influence exercised by those parties in the relevant arena who are in turn important to the employer or client.

The analyst imposes a solution.   A second approach is for the analyst himself or herself to modify—though not replace—the weighting assigned by the employer or client by reference to some overarching philosophical and political conception. The justification usually offered for this approach is that because certain interests, and perhaps philosophies, are typically "underrepresented" in government and politics, and because the analyst is in a better position than most other participants in the process to see or understand or appreciate this problem of underrepresentation, the analyst is duty-bound, or at least permitted, in the name of fairness and democracy, to right the balance.

For instance, some would argue that were it not for policy analysts, efficiency-related criteria would rarely be heeded and that as a consequence, analysts should in effect speak up for the taxpayers whose interests would be squeezed out by better-organized advocacy groups. A related argument is sometimes made that certain conceptions of equity—in particular those having to do with the idea that the beneficiaries of publicly provided goods or services should pay for them—are underrepresented except among policy analysts. (These conceptions of equity normally exclude public expenditures deliberately intended to redistribute wealth among citizens.) Other interests that people sometimes claim are underrepresented and therefore need representation by analysts are future generations, children, people who live outside the jurisdiction making the decisions, ethnic and racial minorities, women, the poor, consumers, and animals and plants (ecological entities).

A variant of this approach introduces the idea of an educational process. Depending on circumstances, the analyst might encourage influential political actors—perhaps including the analyst's boss or principal client—to rethink their existing criteria in the light of facts or arguments the analyst can draw to their attention. In this case, the analyst is responsible for opening up a dialogue, and perhaps for trying to infuse it with reason and insight, but then allows the political process to take over.

Commonly Used Practical Criteria

Not all criteria that come into play in an analysis are part of the evaluative plot line. Some are purely practical and are part of the analytical plot line. These criteria have to do with what happens to an alternative as it moves through the policy adoption and policy-implementation processes.[6] The main ones are legality, political acceptability, robustness under conditions of administrative implementation, and improvability.

Legality.   A feasible policy must not violate constitutional, statutory, or common law rights. However, remember that legal rights are constantly changing and are often ambiguous. It is sometimes worth taking a gamble on a policy that might—or might not—be adjudged illegal when

---

6. I said earlier that criteria apply to outcomes and not to alternatives. However, this statement needs a slight amendment in the case of practical criteria, which apply not to outcomes but to the *prospects* an alternative faces as it goes through the policy adoption and implementation process.

tested in court. (In such cases, advice of counsel is clearly in order to help craft the policy so that its survival chances are enhanced.)

Note, however, that rights alleged to be "natural" or "human" are conceptually quite different from legal rights, despite the semantic similarity—examples are abortion rights or right to life or a woman's right to her own body. Alleged natural or human "rights" are sometimes controversial in that some people would like to have them recognized as rights while others would oppose such recognition.

Political acceptability.   A feasible policy must be politically acceptable, or at least not unacceptable. Political unacceptability is a combination of two things: too much opposition (which may be wide or intense or both) and/or too little support (which may be insufficiently broad or insufficiently intense or both).

Do not take a static view of unacceptability, however. Always ask yourself the question "If my favorite policy solution doesn't look acceptable under current conditions, what would it take to change those conditions?" You might discover that creative political strategizing can open up options that haven't been seriously considered before.

In assessing strategic limitations and possibilities, it will help to make use of various models of the political process. As I observed above, models are based on metaphors, and the ones that are likely to be most valuable in this case are these:

- A complex game in which well-organized and well-positioned minorities enjoy special advantages
- A theater, in which the actors are elected officials who strive, with or without a basis in reality, to create a good appearance—to themselves, to each other, to the critics, and to the audience (whose approval, ultimately, is all-important)
- A marketplace of slogans, symbols, and ideas, with a mix of honorable merchants and hucksters as sellers and a mix of sophisticates and innocents as buyers
- A school in which elected officials learn how to do good policy design work and sometimes share their results and their methods with their classmates

How exactly is one to "make use" of such models? Think of them as conceptual lenses. Observe the relevant political process through each of them in turn, and identify the probable pitfalls and opportunities brought into focus by each.[7]

Robustness and improvability.   Policy ideas that sound great in theory often fail under conditions of actual field implementation. The implementation process has a life of its own. It is acted out through large and inflexible administrative systems and is distorted by bureaucratic interests. Policies that emerge in practice can diverge, even substantially, from policies as designed and adopted. A policy alternative, therefore, should be robust enough so that even if the implementation process does not go very smoothly, the policy outcomes will still prove to be satisfactory.[8]

Some adverse implementation outcomes usually worth worrying about are long delays; capture of program or policy benefits by a relatively undeserving and unintended constituency; excessive budgetary or administrative costs; scandal from fraud, waste, and abuse that undermines political support and embarrasses supporters; and administrative complexities that leave citizens (and program managers) uncertain as to what benefits are available or what regulations must be complied with.

Even the best policy planners cannot get all the details right at the design stage. They should therefore allow room for policy implementers to improve on the original design. The most common vehicle for such improvement is participation in the implementation process by individuals and groups whose expertise or point of view was not included in the design phase. However, note that the openness that makes for improvability can also, by opening the door to hostile political interests, diminish robustness. Hence, a very careful evaluation of the current factual situation—personalities, institutional demands and incentives, political vulnerabilities and so on—is usually in order.

---

7. An analogous procedure was first given prominence by Graham Allison (1971).
8. Robustness under conditions of "deep uncertainty" is sometimes a preeminently important criterion, e.g., for long-term and very risky problems such as global climate change or shifts in the technical and organizational capacity of terrorist movements and cells (Lempert, Popper, and Bankes 2003).

In estimating robustness and improvability, models of bureaucracy can serve as useful conceptual lenses, as suggested above with regard to carrying out political analysis. I find the most useful metaphors about bureaucracy to be these, listed in no particular order:

- An automaton enacting preprogrammed routines ("standard operating procedures," or "SOPs")
- A person in an environment, driven by a will to survive, self-enhancement, and, under some conditions, self-actualization
- A political arena where individuals and factions jockey for influence over the organization's mission, access to its decision systems, and its prerequisites
- A tribe with its own rituals and an array of safeguards against contamination by "outsiders"
- A society of individuals cooperating towards a more-or-less common set of goals—though with various frictions and misunderstandings and some explicit and implicit bargaining over terms
- A structure of roles and interrelationships that are intended to complement one another in a rational division of labor
- An instrument used by "society" for "society's" own objectives

Useful Criteria in Optimization Models

Criteria such as efficiency, equity, political acceptability, and robustness are substantive. But we can think of criteria of a purely formal sort as well. For instance, we can distinguish between criterion values that we wish to maximize, those that must be minimally satisfied, and those for which "more is better."

It is helpful to focus initially on one primary criterion, a *principal objective to be maximized* (or minimized). Typically this principal objective will be the obverse side of your problem definition. For instance, if your problem is that too many families are homeless, then your principal objective would probably be to minimize the number of homeless families. If the problem is that the greenhouse effect is growing too rapidly, a good statement of a principal objective might be "Minimize growth of the greenhouse effect." Naturally, there are other criteria to judge outcomes by, such as costliness, political acceptability, and economic justice, and these should all enter into the final evaluation. However, it is very likely that unless you focus—initially, at least—on a single primary criterion and array others around it, you will find yourself getting very confused. As you get deeper into the analysis, and feel more comfortable with a multiplicity of important objectives, you may wish to drop your emphasis on a primary criterion and work on a more complex "objective function," in the language of mathematical programming.

Linear programming.   A mathematical (and now computer-accessible) technique for optimizing choice when you have a principal objective or an objective function and a scarce stock of resources for maximizing it is called "linear programming" (Stokey and Zeckhauser 1978, chap. 11). Often, at least some of the resources (e.g., the agency budget and the available physical facilities promised by a nonprofit agency) are constrained. Even if the problem is not subject to simple quantitative assessment, analysts often find it useful to take advantage of the logical structure of linear programming to conceptualize their task. The conventional formulation then sounds like this: Maximize this objective (or objective function) subject to such-and-such resource constraints.

Here is an example from the homelessness problem: "Maximize the number of homeless individuals housed on any given night, subject to the constraints of not exceeding $50,000 per night total budgetary cost to Agency X, not putting shelters into Neighborhoods A and B for political reasons, and trying to give 'more' choice to the beneficiary population as to where they will take shelter."

Linguistic clarity.   If it is possible to sort your criteria according to whether they refer to values to be maximized, values that stand as constraints, or values that have a more-is-better quality, keep the different statuses of the criteria in mind. Be conscious of them. You can do this with a simple verbal trick: as appropriate, define your criteria as "Maximize such-and-such value"; "Satisfy such-and-such value constraint"; and "Get more of such-and-such value."

STEP FIVE: PROJECT THE OUTCOMES

Now for each of the alternatives on your current list, project all the outcomes (or impacts) that you or other interested parties might reasonably care about. This is the hardest step in the Eightfold Path. Even veteran policy analysts do not usually do it very well. Not surprisingly, analysts often duck it entirely, disguising their omission by a variety of subterfuges. Hence, the most important advice about this step is simple: Do it.

There are (at least) three great practical as well as psychological difficulties. First, "policy" is about the future, not about the past or the present, but we can never be certain about how the future will unfold, even if we engage it with the best of intentions and the most thoughtful of policy designs.

Second, "Project the outcomes" is another way of saying "Be realistic." Yet, realism is often uncomfortable. Most people prefer optimism. Policy can actually affect people's lives, fortunes, and sacred honor, for better or for worse. Making policy, therefore, imposes a moral burden that is heavier than many people care to acknowledge. Understandably, we would rather believe that our preferred or recommended policy alternative will actually accomplish what we hope and that it will impose fewer costs than we might realistically fear.

Third, there is what is sometimes called "the 51–49 principle." That is, in the thick of the policy fray, we are driven out of pure self-defense to treat 51-percent confidence in our projection as though it deserved 100-percent confidence, with the result that we sometimes mislead not only others but ourselves as well. The first difficulty—namely, that we can never have wholly convincing evidence about the future—compounds the second and third, inasmuch as our wishful thinking is not readily disciplined by reference to empirical demonstrations and proofs.

These cautionary notes notwithstanding, remember that we do not wish to swing toward pessimism either. Realistic projection is our goal.

Extend the Logic of Projection

In this section I discuss, in a very general way, the logic of combining models and evidence to produce usable projections of policy outcomes attached to the various alternatives being considered. The logic is largely that of common sense, but with some important additions.

The first addition is that of metaphor. Policy analysis, as we have seen, makes use of the metaphors behind the models—metaphors such as "bureaucracy as automaton" and "politics as theater" and "this piece of the world as production system"—to yield qualitative insights about important causal relationships. The especially important relationships are those that might afford useful intervention points in complex systems and that present potential pitfalls in policy adoption or implementation processes.

Second, policy analysis uses social science to the degree that it can. A great deal of social science is directed toward answering the question "Is Model X of this piece of the world realistic?" Social scientific studies of this type can often be useful for diagnosing the existence of problems, mapping trends, and deciding whether some seemingly "smart" practice (see Part III) is worth trying to replicate. You should be careful, however, to avoid using the social scientific standard of adequacy for judgments about the realism of a model, for it is quite conservative. In policy analysis the looser, but more appropriate, standard should be whether reliance on a model can lead to better results and avoid worse results than less disciplined guesswork.

Third, policy analysis, as we have seen, uses multiple models. Most social science, in imitation of the hard sciences, looks for "the best" model (and, for some practitioners, "the true" model). Because all models abstract from reality, however, even the best models are never complete. While such abstraction can advance the progress of science, in the world of policy, where real consequences of policy choices are to be experienced by real people, no facet of a problem or the possible alternatives to be adopted can be exempted from analysis. Whatever models *can* be employed to illuminate some important facet of the problem or of the possible outcomes *should* be employed—even if doing so results in an inelegant and ad hoc multiplication of subanalyses.

When it comes to employing multiple models, common sense, unfortunately, is no more enthusiastic than social science. The public debate over whether, or how, to attack Microsoft's dominance in computer software, for instance, featured the company as either a monopolistic rent-seeker or a powerful innovator and promoter of standardization, whereas it clearly has been all these at the same time.

Finally, even when you have embarked on using adequately realistic models of sufficient number and variety, they still need to be used in conjunction with evidence about "initial conditions," or the facts on the ground as they currently exist. Although the projections of many models are not particularly sensitive to initial conditions, some are. These are the models that bear on projections of political acceptability and on the robustness of an alternative to the stresses of the implementation process.

Magnitude Estimates

Projecting outcomes often requires you to think not just about the general direction of an outcome but about the magnitude as well. Typically it's not enough to say, "We expect this program to have a very positive effect on reducing unwanted teenage pregnancies." Instead, you'd want to say, "We expect this program to reduce by one hundred to three hundred the number of unwanted teenage pregnancies per year in this community over the next five years."

Sometimes a single-point estimate of your best guess about the degree of magnitude will suffice. But in other cases you should provide a range.

Break-Even Estimates

A convenient way to handle uncertainty in estimation is with *break-even estimates.* These calculations use what you do know or can reasonably assume in order to "frame the residual uncertainty" in a way that is meaningful for decision making.

Suppose, for instance, that some youth-guidance-oriented policy meant to reduce incarceration of juveniles is under consideration and has known costs of $1 million, but the level of effectiveness is speculative. You build a frame for the remaining uncertainty in these four steps:

1. Locate the point of minimum acceptable effectiveness given the costs. Ask, "What is the minimum level of effectiveness this policy would have to achieve in order to justify our spending $1 million?" Your answer: "Different observers have different opinions about how much avoiding an incarceration is worth, but leaving that aside and going with my own values, I'd say that $300 a year, or a 15-per-

cent reduction, is the minimum I would accept given the expenditure of $1 million." [9]

2. Referring back to your model of the processes that create the problem and hold it in place, ask, "What new processes, or changes in old ones, could conceivably produce this level of effectiveness?" This is largely a qualitative analysis. The answer might be "Based on previous documentation of how the guidance process works, we can safely say that it works in different ways with different sorts of kids—when it works at all, that is. It can provide about half the kids more constructive life choices; in about a quarter of the cases it works through heightening the (realistic) perception of punishment; and in about a quarter of cases we are just crossing our fingers."

3. Assess how likely (or unlikely) it is that the processes for improvement thus identified will actually produce the required—that is, the break-even—level of effectiveness. It is particularly helpful to ask whether the break-even level (15 percent in this case) looks like a plausible number given what is known or assumed about the effectiveness in similar circumstances of similar sorts of interventions. If the number is implausibly high, you might then go on to ask whether special circumstances of some sort might be at work in this case to help achieve it. Note that in this and the previous step you must rely on what we might think of as "theory," or self-conscious and evidence-based reasoning about the way causal processes work. Typically, these are the weakest links in the chain of policy-analytic reasoning. That is why it is particularly important—and particularly difficult—to take this step as thoughtfully, self-critically, and responsibly as possible.

4. Estimate the probability of failure and the political and other costs of having to accept failure—asking yourself whether they would be tolerable should they be incurred.

---

9. Some people speak of "switchpoint analysis" and would refer to the 15 percent here as the switchpoint at which a decision maker would switch from a favorable view of this policy to an unfavorable view or vice versa. Others refer to "threshold analysis" and would call the 15-percent figure the threshold level of effectiveness we would need to assume in order to justify choosing this alternative.

I find break-even analysis to be intuitive and commonsensical. But not everyone does. In the hope that it may be helpful to illustrate the process in terms of some policy domains other than youth guidance, I offer two more examples:

- Policy X for establishing a chain of wildlife refuges looks like an excellent choice to implement a broader conservation agenda, provided that the funding really comes through as planned. But it might not, because federal grant-in-aid resources may not be forthcoming, or the governor may give the policy lower priority than she now promises, or some development interests that have their eye on two of the designated sites may find a way to block it. You interview your client, a state environmental agency director, and determine that she likes the program so much that she is willing to go for it if it has at least a 50–50 chance of working out. Your analysis can then focus her attention on why, after considerable research, you have concluded that it has a somewhat better (or somewhat worse) chance than 50–50, even though you would find it impossible to specify exactly how much better (or worse).

- Building a new stadium for the Hometown Heroes looks like a good idea, given the nature of the costs and benefits, if average daily attendance turns out to be no less than 10,000. That's the break-even attendance figure for you and the relevant decision makers. Then it's up to them to decide, first, how confident they are that this break-even level will be reached, and then, whether that degree of confidence is enough to warrant making an affirmative decision. You would then organize your presentation of facts and opinions to focus on these two key issues.[10]

Here is a semantic suggestion for making use of the logic of break-even analysis. Assuming for the moment that benefits are uncertain while

---

10. A special case of break-even estimation is a fortiori estimation. If you hypothesize worst-case estimates of all important parameters that are still uncertain and the policy alternative still satisfies your decision criterion, the alternative would, a fortiori, prove satisfactory even if more careful estimates were to be more favorable. In that case, the more careful estimates are unnecessary. See MacRae and Whittington 1997 on a fortiori analysis (218–219) and, more generally, on the question of precision versus approximation in projecting outcomes (209–224).

costs are not, ask yourself these two questions: (1) "Given what I know for sure about the costs of this alternative, what is the minimum help we need to get from Condition X to ensure adequately offsetting benefits?" and (2) "How reasonable is it to believe that Condition X will actually produce that minimum?" The first question could also be framed in terms of known benefits and the conditions that would yield minimally acceptable costs.

Try Sensitivity Analysis

Which uncertainties are the most important, in the sense that relatively small changes in what you believe would cause you to change your mind about how desirable some alternative might be? By a process known as "sensitivity analysis," you can discover these "most important" uncertainties. The procedures are somewhat technical (Morgan and Henrion 1990, chap. 8), but the intuition behind them is simple. Consider the several assumptions you have made on the way to your conclusion and suppose that each of them is somewhat mistaken. Now ask yourself: "How big a mistake can I afford in this assumption before this analysis is in really big trouble?" The smaller the affordable mistake, the more "sensitive" is your analysis to the particular assumption.[11] (For a good example of sensitivity analysis, see Appendix A.)

It is not hard to examine these assumptions one at a time. But what if they pile up such that you are "somewhat" wrong on two or three or four assumptions all at once? This situation is dealt with by a technique called "Monte Carlo simulation," which begins by recognizing that each assumption is in itself probabilistic and then combines the probabilities behind the assumptions to create a new set of probabilities about how the combination of assumptions will turn out. You can then say something like this: "Given the many possible scenarios that might occur, there is an 82-percent chance that the actual scenario would exceed our break-even requirement."[12]

---

11. Of course you could be wrong in ways that protect your results as well as defeat them.

12. For further details, see Morgan and Henrion 1990, chap. 8. You can use the commercially available (and very user-friendly) Crystal Ball program to run Monte Carlo simulations.

Confront the Optimism Problem

Great ventures require optimism. Because even small ventures by government can affect so many lives, they are in their own way "great." Hence, some "realistic" optimism is beneficial. But how do you guard against excessive optimism?

Scenario writing.   What scenarios might cause the proposal to fail to produce the desired outcome (e.g., solving or sufficiently mitigating the policy problems)? Do not create such scenarios from whole cloth—be realistic. And yet, let your imagination run a little, so that you have a good chance of thinking of the most dangerous possibilities. In particular, think about the dangers of the implementation process, political and otherwise. Scenario writing also benefits from thinking about possible failures from a vantage point in the future looking backward. Consider the following scenarios:

- In a health or safety regulatory program, the scientific or technical knowledge necessary to produce rational and legally defensible standards may prove to be lacking. As a result, five years from now, symbolic politics, corruption, industry capture, or excessive regulatory zeal will have filled the vacuum.
- Time passes, and budgetary resources and political support that were once available slip away under the impact of electoral change and shifts in the economy. A terrorist-identification program, begun under nurturant leaders and accompanied by editorialists' applause, will have become consolidated with another program, then taken over by a different bureaucratic unit, and eventually will have disappeared.
- A successful state program designed to furnish technical assistance to extremely poor rural counties will have added a mandate to aid many not-so-poor urban counties, with the result that scarce program resources will have been dissipated and squandered. (I call this scenario "piling on"; see Bardach 1977).
- A program that subsidizes research and development of "fish protein concentrate," intended as a cheap and nutritious food additive, is launched with great fanfare. Five years from now it will have been

stalled, permanently, by the Food and Drug Administration, which will not have been able to assimilate this product into its standard operating procedures for regulatory review.

Notice that these scenarios are written in the future perfect tense. This encourages concreteness, which is a helpful stimulant to the imagination (Weick 1979, 195–200). It often helps your scenario-writing to start with a list of adverse implementation outcomes, conjuring up one or more scenarios about how each of these might occur. Remember the list of such outcomes embodied in the scenarios just described: long delays; "capture" of program or policy benefits by a relatively undeserving and unintended constituency; excessive budgetary or administrative costs; scandal from fraud, waste, and abuse that undermines political support and embarrasses supporters; and administrative complexities that leave citizens (and program managers) uncertain as to what benefits are available or what regulations must be complied with.

The other-guy's-shoes heuristic.   Imagine yourself in the other guy's shoes. Say to yourself, "If I were X, how would I act?" And then proceed to crawl into X's mind and play out, in your own mind, what X might do. Do this systematically for each of the important stakeholders or other affected parties. The value of this exercise is that you will discover them to be adapting in surprising ways to the new policy situation you might be creating—and with results that might cause trouble for your policy design.

For example, under chemical right-to-know laws, workers must be told what substances they have been exposed to, and they may examine health records maintained by employers. If you were a worker, how might you use this law? Might you use the information to quit your present job? To demand a higher wage or more protective equipment? To sue your employer or put pressure on your union representative?

And how would your union representative react to such pressure? Might this pressure make the representative's job harder—or perhaps easier in some way?

Now, suppose you were an employer. Given what you expect your workers to do, you would face incentives to make adaptations or countermoves. Might you stop keeping all health records not explicitly required by law? Or continue keeping records but permit doctors to perform only selected lab tests? And if you were a worker and saw your employer doing these things, what countermoves would you make?

Not all the moves and countermoves of players wearing the other guy's shoes will necessarily lead to trouble for the policy alternative you are evaluating. Many such adaptation sequences may prove to be helpful, in the sense that they may help society adjust to the changes set in motion by the new policy. At some point in the 1970s, the Federal Trade Commission (FTC) attacked the problem of retailers evading implied warranty obligations for defective products by selling installment debts to banks and other collectors that had no duty, under the so-called holder-in-due-course doctrine, to fix the product or to refrain from collecting on the installment debt. The FTC solution was, in effect, to abolish the protections of the holder-in-due-course doctrine. Banks complained that they did not want to go into the toaster repair business. But if you put yourself in the shoes of a bank manager suddenly obliged to become a toaster repairer, might you not have thought of contracting out your repair obligations to repair specialists, or perhaps arranging not to buy installment debts from retailers who you believed could not be relied upon to make good on their implied warranties?

Undesirable side effects.   Analysts are often cautioned to think about *unanticipated consequences.* But this term is not appropriate, for it is often used to refer to perfectly anticipatable, though undesirable, side effects. Here are some common undesirable but foreseeable side effects in public programs:

- *Moral hazard* increases. That is, your policy has the effect of insulating people from the consequences of their actions. For example, increasing the size of unemployment benefits has the side effect of blunting the incentives to search for a replacement job.
- *Overregulation* in the health and safety areas backfires. One possible adverse result of setting health or safety standards "too high" and enforcing them "too uniformly" is that you increase private-sector costs beyond some desirable optimum. For instance, given most people's private preferences for safety, imposing auto bumper standards that cost some $25 per vehicle but that have only trivial

effects on improving vehicle crashworthiness would not pass a conventional benefit-cost test.

A second adverse result of overregulation might be that you inadvertently cause a shift away from the regulated activity into some other activity that—perversely—is less safe or less healthful. For instance, some observers argue that overregulating the safety features of nuclear power production has caused a shift toward coal, which they argue is much more hazardous than nuclear power.

- *Rent-seekers*—that is, interests looking out for profitable niches protected from full competition—distort the program to serve their own interests. It is not inevitable that suppliers of goods and services to the government, including civil servants, will find ways to capture "rents," but it often happens (e.g., with many defense contractors). Rent-seeking also occurs in less obvious ways (e.g., when some regulated firms successfully lobby for regulations that impose much higher compliance costs on their competitors than on themselves).

The ethical costs of optimism.   It is hard to overstate the importance of worrying about the possible adverse side effects of otherwise "good" policies, not to mention the possibility that even intended main benefits may fail to materialize under many circumstances (see the chapter on "Assessing Your Ignorance" in Behn and Vaupel 1982). The ethical policy analyst always poses the question, "If people actually were to follow my advice, what might be the costs of my having been wrong, and who would have to bear them?" And keep in mind that the analyst typically is *not* one of the parties who have to bear the costs of his or her mistakes.

Construct an Outcomes Matrix

The step of projecting outcomes leads you into a dense thicket of information. You will not want to present or discuss all of it in your final report. But at any point along the way you may need to be able to stand back and assess complex and uncertain scenarios for up to eight or ten basic alternatives, combined with their principal variants. A convenient way to get an overview of all this information is to display it in an "outcomes matrix." A smaller version of such a matrix might also prove useful in your final report.

The typical outcomes matrix format arrays your policy alternatives down the rows and your evaluative criteria across the columns. Any cell, then, contains the projected outcome of the row alternative as assessed by reference to the column criterion. If you cannot fill in the cell with a quantitatively expressed description of the projected outcome, you might settle for a verbal descriptor such as "very good" or a symbolic descriptor such as + or -.

Table I-1 is an example I created a few years ago in order to compare projected outcomes of three alternative systems for periodically inspecting California's 10 million automobiles for smog-control compliance. In this example, Baker, Smith, and Jones—analysts working for three different government agencies and with somewhat opposed policy views—are making rather different projections of outcomes for each of these alternatives. I record their rival projections in the cells where they differed.[13]

A common error that occurs in labeling the criteria columns in such a matrix is to fail to indicate what value is at stake and in what dimensions the measurement is being done. For instance, if you are assessing a rental subsidy program and you enter a plus sign in a column labeled "Landlord/tenant relations," the reader may not know whether you think relations will become more harmonious, more confrontational, less dominated by landlords, less dominated by tenants, or something else. It is not sufficient that your surrounding text makes your intention clear; the matrix label itself must be informative. In my illustrative matrix, I did not simply write *cleanup* or *cost* or *time*. Within the space constraints I tried to indicate the metric and the desired direction in which it should move. In many cases it helps to insert *maximize* or *minimize* in the criterion label.

You can simplify the mass of information you need to display and assimilate in your outcomes matrix (or in any other format) if you

---

13. For other examples, see Tables 9-4, 9-5, 9-8, and 9-9 in Stokey and Zeckhauser 1978. See also the discussion in Weimer and Vining 1999, 282–289, and their sample matrices on 285–313.

TABLE I-1	**Outcomes Projected by Three Different Analysts for Three Alternative Fleet Inspection Systems**

CRITERIA

ALTERNATIVES	Maximize needed cleanup (percentage attained)	Minimize cost per ton of pollution reduced ($)	Minimize consumer time (minutes)	Reduce test cost to vehicle owner ($)
IM 240[a]	Baker: 100 Smith: 0	Baker:<SC Smith: Millions	Jones: 60 Smith: >60	Jones:<SC Baker:>SC
Modified Smog Check[b]	Baker: 50 Smith: 0	Baker: Thousands Smith: Millions	Jones: 75 Smith: 75	Smith: 35
Remote Sensing[c]	Baker: 0 Smith: 100	Baker: Millions Smith: 200	Consensus: 0 for most drivers	Consensus: 0 for most owners

Note: The Smog Check (SC) system involved biennial inspections at the time of vehicle re-registration in any one of several thousand approved service stations.

a. Would have required biennial inspections using more sophisticated testing machinery at any one of many fewer centralized and specialized testing facilities.

b. Would have added additional tests and strengthened enforcement procedures in selected areas of the Central Valley and the South Coast air basin.

c. An emerging technology that would simply monitor cars from roadside vans and initiate enforcement measures against those determined to be out of compliance.

eliminate information about outcomes that will be the same for all the alternatives. This omission is particularly useful if the common outcomes are ambiguous or uncertain: you will be spared the trouble of having to make the difficult projections involved.

STEP SIX: CONFRONT THE TRADE-OFFS

It sometimes happens that one of the policy alternatives under consideration is expected to produce a better outcome than any of the other alternatives with regard to every single evaluative criterion. In that case—called "dominance"—there are no trade-offs among the alternatives. Usually, though, you are less fortunate, and you must clarify the trade-offs between outcomes associated with different policy options for the sake of your client and/or audience.

The most common trade-off is between money and a good or service received by some proportion of the citizenry, such as extending library hours from 8 p.m. till 10 p.m., weighed against a cost of $200,000 annually. Another common tradeoff, especially in regulatory policies, involves weighing privately borne costs (a company's installing pollution abatement equipment) against social benefits (improved health and the protection of forests).

As economics teaches us, trade-offs occur at the margin. Trade-off analysis tells us something like this: "If we spend an extra X dollars for an extra unit of Service Y, we can get an extra Z units of good outcome." This kind of analysis puts the decision maker in the position to answer the question "Does society (or do you) value Z more or less than X?" and then to follow the obvious implication of the answer (if yes, decide for another unit of Y; if no, don't).

A linguistic device to help you keep focused on the margin is frequent use of the word *extra*. Note that this word appears three times in the example analysis in the preceding paragraph.

Some units of Service Y can be purchased only in "lumps" larger than one—sometimes much larger. Consider transportation services provided by highways and bridges. Y might be one passenger trip from A to B, but most transportation construction projects (highway enlargements, new bridge crossings) can be undertaken only for minimum bundles of Y that run into the thousands of trips. Or suppose that a police chief must choose one of two "lumpy" alternatives, such as $1 million per year for more overtime on the night shift or $250,000 (annualized) for more rapid replacement of police cars. The first alternative is lumpy because the police union insists on a minimum overtime rate for all 150 officers on the shift, and the second is lumpy because the auto supplier charges much less per vehicle after some threshold number of vehicles. If, say, the projected decrease in burglaries from increased overtime were 200 per year and that from newer vehicles were 50, the trade-off confronting the decision maker at the margin is an extra $5,000 per extra burglary prevented. In this case the "margin" is a lumpy 150 burglaries and $750,000.

(Criteria other than burglary prevention and cost efficiency would, of course, be relevant to this problem.)

Establish Commensurability

Suppose some Alternative A_1 stacks up very well on Criterion C_1, moderately well on C_2, and poorly on C_3. And suppose that A_2 stacks up in the opposite way. We can choose between the two alternatives only if we can weight the importance of the criteria and if we can express their relative weights in units that are commensurable across the criteria. As you may have heard, money is everybody's favorite candidate for the commensurable metric. Using money as the metric is a very good idea, and it often works much better than one might imagine. For instance, even the "value" of life can sometimes be reasonably well described in the metric "willingness to pay X dollars for a reduction in the risk of death by Y percent a year," or something like it.

However, there are limits to the money metric and to commensurability as well. In order to reach a summary judgment as to how much political equality to give up in a political redistricting case, for instance, in exchange for how much more African-American voter power, it seems impossible even to state the trade-off in meaningful terms. In general, this problem is known as the "multiattribute problem." In some deep sense it is logically insoluble, although some heuristics are available to help trim it down to its minimally irreducible size (Stokey and Zeckhauser 1978, 117–133; MacRae and Whittington 1997, 201–203).[14]

Break-even analysis revisited.   We have seen how break-even analysis can help you both to focus on which residual uncertainties you have to estimate and to frame the terms in which that estimate must be given ("We have to believe Alternative A_1 will produce at least X results in order

---

14. One potentially misleading heuristic has the analyst creating a score for each alternative with respect to each criterion and then manipulating the scores arithmetically. It is easy to get the arithmetic right, but it is often hard to come up with scoring procedures that are not at some level arbitrary (e.g., anchored against some arbitrarily defined level of excellence or its opposite).

to justify choosing it"). We turn now to how break-even analysis can also help solve commensurability problems.

Consider those policy areas, such as safety regulation, where we are often implicitly trading off dollars against risks to life. It might be supposed that in order to assess these proposals, you would have to decide what a human life is *really worth*—a task many of us, quite understandably, are unwilling to perform. The task is made somewhat more tractable, however, if you work with quantitative estimates and apply break-even analysis. Suppose, for instance, you are considering whether or not to impose on the auto industry a new design standard that will improve safety and save an estimated twenty-five lives per year every year into the indefinite future. The cost of meeting the standard is estimated at $50 million per year indefinitely. The trade-off at the margin appears to be, therefore, "$2 million per life." But you don't have to answer the question "What's a human life really worth?" in order to make at least some sense of this decision. You do have to answer the question, "Is a statistical life (that is, the life of an unknown individual 'drawn' in a random manner from some population, rather than a named person's life) worth at least $2 million?" That is a break-even analysis sort of question. For reasons best known to yourself, it may be obvious to you that a statistical life surely is—or isn't. And while it's very difficult to decide whether the worth of a statistical life falls on one or the other side of some monetary boundary, it's a lot less difficult than coming up with a point value.

Even this sort of trade-off calculation is troubling to many people, and some find it morally repugnant. Unfortunately, repugnant or not, it is in a sense inevitable. Whatever position you take on the auto safety design standard described, you are by implication also taking a position on the dollars/risk-to-life trade-off: if you favor the standard, you implicitly believe the trade-off is worthwhile, whereas if you oppose it, you don't. Fortunately, this logical implication has its uses. You may in many circumstances quite sensibly prefer to rely on your "intuition" rather than on some complicated systematic method. Once you have reached your conclusion based on intuition, though, you can "check" your intuition by asking yourself, "Since the implication of my policy choice is that I value X as being worth at least (or at most) thus-and-such, do I really believe that?"

Focus on Outcomes

A common pitfall in confronting trade-offs is to think and speak of the trade-offs as being across *alternatives* rather than across projected *outcomes* (e.g., "trading off twenty foot-patrol police officers in the late night hours against a lower-maintenance-cost fleet of police vehicles"). Although there is such a trade-off, you'll see, with a second's thought, that you can't do anything at all with it. Both alternatives must first be converted into outcomes before genuine trade-offs can be confronted. Thus, the competing outcomes might be fifty (plus or minus . . .) burglaries per year prevented by the police versus a savings of $300,000 in fleet maintenance.

Simplify the Comparison Process

Do what you can to simplify the process of comparing alternatives and focusing on the critical trade-offs.

Eliminate weaker alternatives.   First, eliminate any alternative that is clearly dominated by at least one other alternative. Second, look for alternatives that *would* be dominated if you weighted one criterion (or more) rather less heavily than most of the other criteria. Upon reflection, you might decide that this criterion (and possibly others as well) *should* be weighted this low, and so it, too, can be dropped from further consideration.

Pay special attention to the alternative of simply letting present trends continue. If it has not been dropped by this point in the analysis, now is the time to check if it is sufficiently dominated by other alternatives to justify discarding it.

Compare to a base case.   Even if you drop "letting present trends continue" as a reasonable alternative, you might still want to retain the set of outcomes that you have projected for it as a benchmark against which to compare other sets of projected outcomes. Such a benchmark set is often called a "base case." Using a base case as a benchmark is helpful almost apart from what it is. You may wish to use other projections as base cases besides—or in addition to—"letting present trends continue." Other possibly illuminating base cases are these:

- "The likely outcome if we don't manage to head off what the governor's office [or some other powerful faction] is planning . . ."
- "Our ideal set of outcomes if political conditions were just a bit more favorable . . ."
- "The worst-case scenario which we have to prevent practically at any cost . . ."

If you decide to use a base case as a benchmark, you should probably make another outcomes matrix in which each cell entry appraises the projected outcome against its projected base case counterpart. Of course, you may wish to construct your original outcomes matrix in this fashion to begin with.

STEP SEVEN: DECIDE!

This step appears in the Eightfold Path as a check on how well you have done your work up to this point. Even though you personally may not be the decision maker, you should at this point pretend that you are. Then, decide what to do based on your own analysis. If you find this decision difficult or troublesome, the reason may be that you have not clarified the trade-offs sufficiently, or that you have not said quite enough about the probability of serious implementation problems emerging (or not emerging), or that a crucial cost estimate is still too fuzzy and uncertain, or that you have not approximated carefully enough the elasticity of some important demand curve, and so on.

Think of it this way: Unless you can convince *yourself* of the plausibility of some course of action, you probably won't be able to convince your client—and rightly so.

Of course, when you tell your story to your client or any other audience, you may not think it appropriate to make reference to your own decision. You might, instead, simply limit your story to a clarification of the relevant trade-offs and leave the decision completely up to the audience.

Apply the Twenty-Dollar-Bill Test

You should at this point subject your favored policy alternative to the "twenty-dollar-bill test." The name of this test is based on an old joke making fun of economists. Two friends are walking down the street when one stops to pick something up. "What about that—a twenty-dollar bill!" he says. "Couldn't be," says the other, an economist. "If it were, somebody would have picked it up already." The analogy is this: *If your favorite policy alternative is such a great idea, how come it's not happening already?* The most common sources of failure on this test are neglecting to consider the resistance of bureaucratic and other stakeholders in the status quo, and the lack of an entrepreneur in the relevant policy environment who has the incentive to pick up what seems like a great idea and see it through. Failure on this test is not fatal, of course. Just keep fiddling until you invent a variant of your basic idea that will pass.

STEP EIGHT: TELL YOUR STORY

After many iterations of all the above steps—redefining your problem, reconceptualizing your alternatives, reconsidering your criteria, reassessing your projections, re-evaluating the trade-offs—you are ready to tell your story to some audience. The audience might be your client, or it might be broader. It might be hostile, or it might be friendly.

Apply the Grandma Bessie Test

Before proceeding further, you need another little reality check. Suppose your Grandma Bessie, who is intelligent but not very sophisticated politically, asks you about your work. You say you are a "policy analyst working for . . ." She says, "What's that?" You explain that you've been working on "the problem of . . ." She says, "So, what's the answer?" You have one minute to offer a coherent, down-to-earth explanation before her eyes glaze over. If you feel yourself starting to hem and haw, you haven't really understood your own conclusions at a deep enough level to make sense to others, and probably not to yourself either. Back to the drawing board until you get it straight.

Now consider the possibility that someone might actually wish to base a real decision or a policy proposal on your analysis. (It's been known to happen.) Even if you, as an analyst, would not have to deal directly with such a tough audience as Grandma Bessie and her kin (including, of course, Grandpa Max), it's likely that someone will have to do so. At the very least, therefore, you'll have to be able to explain your basic story to someone in sufficiently simple and down-to-earth terms that that someone will be able to carry on with the task of public, democratic education.

Gauge Your Audience(s)

Assuming you've passed the Grandma Bessie test, identify and assess the likely audience(s) that are more sophisticated and involved than Grandma Bessie.

First comes your client, the person or persons whose approval you need most—your hierarchical superior(s), perhaps, or those who are funding your work. What is the relationship between you and your client? What you say and how you say it should depend a great deal on whether your relationship is long-term and on whether it is carried on face-to-face. In particular, how easy will it be for you to correct any misunderstandings that might arise?

Next, think about the larger political environment. Who do you think will "use" the analysis and for what purpose(s)? Will anyone pick up your results for use in an advocacy context? Would you regard this use of your results as desirable? Desirable if certain advocates use your work and undesirable if others do so? Do you want to do anything to "segregate" your policy advice by the type of audience you might want it to reach—or not reach? Are you, perhaps inadvertently, using scare words that will alienate certain audiences?

If you are making a clear recommendation, make sure you raise and rebut possible objections to it that might occur to various important audiences. Also make sure that you compare it to what you or others might regard as the next best course of action, so as to be ready to show why yours is better.

Consider What Medium to Use

You can tell your story in written or in oral form. In either case, communicate simply and clearly. The guiding principle is that other things being equal, shorter is always better. In written presentations, good subheadings and graphics can make reading and comprehension easier. Visual aids such as flip charts, overhead transparencies, and computer-based slide projections often help in oral presentations.

Oral presentations require practice, self-discipline, and a little knowledge of some basic principles. The most basic of the basic principles are these: speak *very slowly and distinctly*; speak loudly enough to be heard throughout the room, even over distracting noises; speak in a lower register, which tends to increase perceived trustworthiness and credibility; do not fidget, but don't stand like a stick either; make lots of eye contact with audience members and, in doing so, don't favor one side of the room over another. Speaking slowly and distinctly is probably harder than you think—and more important, too.

Give Your Story a Logical Narrative Flow

Your story's flow should be designed with the reader's (or listener's) needs and interests and abilities in mind. In both written and oral presentations, it should be evident to the audience what motivates the entire analysis. Therefore it is best to open with a statement of the problem your analysis addresses.[15]

It is also important to *motivate* the more detailed steps in the flow of the analysis, that is, the sections, paragraphs, and sentences. Most readers will look for the motivation of any element in what immediately precedes it, which makes it important to avoid lengthy digressions. For these reasons, be wary of sections you are tempted to label "Background." Similarly, the phrases "Before turning to . . ." and "It is first necessary to explain/understand the history of . . ." are usually signs of undigested material. Many readers will be alert to these danger signs, so you should be, too. Policy analysis, remember, is about the future. Perhaps surprisingly—it is often not obvious how, or whether—history affects the future, but the burden should be on the writer or speaker to show exactly how this effect will come about.

A common, though not uniformly applicable, organizing framework is to begin with a good problem definition and then to treat each alternative you consider as a major section. Within each such section, you

---

15. An unusually fine manual on how to give slide-based oral briefings is published by the RAND Corporation (1994).

project the probable outcome(s) of implementing the alternative and assess how likely such outcome(s) are in the light of some causal model and associated evidence. Following these discussions, you review and summarize the alternative outcomes and discuss their trade-offs. Note that in this framework there is no special discussion of criteria. However, sometimes an explicit discussion of criteria is important; it might appear either just before or just after the presentation of the alternatives and their associated outcomes.

Some Common Pitfalls

Following the Eightfold Path too closely.   Sometimes it helps to structure your narrative flow as though you were leading the reader by the hand down the Eightfold Path. But usually this approach is a mistake. The purpose of the Eightfold Path, remember, is to help you *think through* a complicated problem. It is not at all necessary to use it in telling the story, though some aspects of it sometimes help.

Compulsive qualifying.   Don't interrupt the flow of an argument in order to display all the qualifications and uncertainties about some particular element in the argument. A linguistic way around this pitfall is to use adjectives or adjective phrases such as *most, on average*, and *more often than not* to state the generality, and then to return to the exceptions in the next section. (Or, if the exceptions and qualifications really can't wait, try a parenthetical sentence or a footnote.)

Showing off all your work.   Don't include every fact you ever learned in the course of your research. Even if you've done a good and thorough job of research and analysis, most of what you have learned will prove to be irrelevant by the time you're finished. That is, you will have succeeded in focusing your own attention on what is really important and in downplaying what only appeared important at the beginning. You don't usually need to take your reader on the same wandering course you were obliged to follow.

Listing without explaining.   Should you list every alternative policy that you intend to analyze in the report before you actually get around to providing the analysis? Such a list is a good thing when the alternatives are not numerous, when they are all taken seriously either by you or by your audience, and when they will prepare the reader's mind for the detailed assessment that will follow. However, if you have many alternatives to consider, the reader will forget what's on the list, and if some of the alternatives turn out to be easily dismissed upon closer scrutiny, you'll simply have been setting up straw men and wasting the reader's mental energy.

Similarly, be cautious about listing every evaluative criterion of interest before coming to the assessment of the alternatives being considered. Usually—though not always—there is not much to be said in a separate section about criteria that can't be better said when you're actually writing the assessment sections.

Spinning a mystery yarn.   Start with the conclusion, the bottom line, the absolutely most interesting point you intend to make. Then explain all the reasoning and evidence that you hope will make your audience reach the same conclusions you have reached. In short, follow the opposite strategy from that which a novelist would follow.

Inflating the style.   Avoid the pomposity and circumlocutions of the bureaucratic and the academic styles. (Essential reading: George Orwell, *Politics and the English Language.*) Also to be avoided: a chatty, insider's style—e.g., "We all understand what creeps our opponents are, don't we?"

Structure Your Report

Unless the report is short, begin with an executive summary.

If your report is over fifteen to twenty pages long, say, a table of contents is often helpful. If there are many tables and figures, either in the text or in the appendixes, a contents list of these can be helpful as well. Detailed technical information or calculations should appear in appendixes rather than in the text. However, enough technical information, and reasoning, should appear in the text itself to persuade the reader that you really do know what you're talking about and that your argument is at least credible.

Use headings and subheadings to help keep the reader oriented and to break up large bodies of text; make sure your formatting (caps, italics, boldface, indentation) is compatible with, and indeed supports, the logical hierarchy of your argument.

Table format. Current professional practice is very poor with respect to the formatting of tables. Do not imitate it but strive to improve it. Every table (or figure) should have a number (Table 1, for instance, or Figure 3-A) and a title. The title should be intelligible; it is often useful to have the title describe the main point to be learned from the table (e.g., "Actual Risks of Drinking and Driving Rise Rapidly with Number of Drinks— but Are Greatly Underestimated by College Students"). Each row and column in a table must be labeled, and the label should be interpretable without too much difficulty.

Normally, a table either is purely descriptive or is designed to demonstrate some causal relationship. In the latter case, it is usually desirable to create a table that makes a single point (or at most two) and that can stand alone without need of much explanation in the surrounding text. It is usually better to use two or three small tables to make two or three points than to construct one massive table and then try to explain its contents by means of the text that surrounds it.

Tables usually require footnotes, and there should almost always be a source note at the bottom. Sometimes the footnotes refer to data sources used to make the table, and sometimes they attempt to clarify the meaning of the row or column labels, which are necessarily abbreviated.

References and sources. Include a listing of references and sources at the end of the presentation. Books and articles should be cited in academic style (alphabetical order by author). The main point is to provide bibliographic help to curious and/or skeptical readers who want to track down references for themselves. There are several acceptable styles, but a good model is the one used in the book review section of the *Journal of Policy Analysis and Management*, which is simple and direct.

The current trend is toward "scientific citation" in lieu of footnote references in the text. That is, cite the author's last name and year of publication in parentheses in the text; the reader then consults the references section at the end for the full citation. If you follow this practice, the reference section should list the author(s) and the year *before* the title of the work and publication details. Sometimes you will want to include a page number in the parenthetical citation as well.

Legal citation style is quite different. If most of the references are legal, then it is advisable to cite all references in bottom-of-page footnotes. However, you can keep the scientific citation format within the footnote.

Notes are easier to read if they appear on the same page as the referenced text—that is, if you display them as footnotes rather than as endnotes.

Using a Memo Format

If your analysis is to be delivered in a memo, you should present it within a standard memo format, as follows:

[Date]
To: [Recipient name(s), official position(s)]
From: [Your name, position. Sign or initial next to or above your name.]
Subject: [Brief and grammatically correct description of the subject]

[First sentence or two should remind recipient of the fact that she or he asked you for a memo on this subject, and why. Alternatively, you could explain why you are submitting this memo on this subject to the recipient at this time.]
[If memo is long, you might open and close with a summary paragraph or two. If you open with a long summary, the closing summary can be short.]
[If memo is long, consider breaking it up with subheads.]

Develop a Press Release

Most policy analyses do not become the subjects of press releases or of radio or television sound bites, but some do. Others become candidates for such treatment, and all can profit, even in their extended form, from the analyst's reflecting on how to condense the essential message. Hence, it will probably serve an analytical purpose, and sometimes a political purpose, if you sketch out a press release and/or a few ideas for sound bites. You might also wish to think strategically and defensively to see how an opponent might characterize your work in a press release or sound bite.

ASSEMBLING EVIDENCE

Consider the problem confronting a researcher preparing an analysis of water pollution control programs for Blue Lake. He knows there is a dirty lake; that there is federal, state, and local legislation directed toward the end of cleaning up the lake (or preventing it from getting much dirtier); and that there is a state environmental protection office in the area that has something to do with administering some or all of the relevant antipollution policies or programs. But the researcher needs to know more. He needs to map the present policies and programs, their political environment, the way the bureaucracies function to implement them, and the criteria by which experts and nonprofessionals evaluate them. He also needs to make some decisions about how he himself will evaluate them. Then he needs to learn what data are relevant to these criteria and figure out how to obtain these data. If he is planning to recommend changes in existing programs, he must develop the evidence that will permit him to make reasonable projections of the likely outcomes. In addition, he must learn what sort of changes the present set of relevant actors might be prepared to make or are capable of making.

These are large challenges, but the researcher's resources in time, energy, money, and the goodwill of potential informants and interviewers are probably not at all large. Moreover, he would like to finish the study in no more than six months, let us say, and he does not want to waste the first five months simply getting his bearings. Where is he to begin? And once begun, how is he to proceed efficiently?

GETTING STARTED

The very first step is simple: Start with what you know. This injunction may seem self-evident or trivial or both. In fact, it is common for people to act in contradiction of it. Confronted by a new and challenging research task, they expect to flounder anxiously for a few weeks or months. And behold they do, for feeling stupid makes you so. Rarely is this necessary, however. A few facts, or even vague recollections, plus some intelligent reasoning can usually move the project onto firm footing surprisingly quickly. Suppose, for example, you are asked to do a policy analysis of "the future of the Wichahissic bituminous coal industry," a subject as remote from your interest or previous experience as galactic spectroscopy. You might take stock by writing a memo to yourself as follows:

- I was probably asked to do this study because someone thinks the future of the Wichahissic bituminous coal industry is pretty bleak or else because it is looking up. If the former, the results will probably be used to justify some sort of government subsidy; if the latter, the results will be used for promotional purposes by the industry itself or by local merchants whose livelihood depends on the health of the industry.
- The future of any industry depends in part on market demand. The demand for coal has probably been declining, partly due to the availability of substitute fuels.
- Maybe there are high production costs that imperil the health of the industry. Could it be that coal-mining technology is underdeveloped? If so, why? Perhaps the coalfields are running out and the technology has not been developed to handle poor, as opposed to rich, deposits.
- There were a lot of miners' strikes a few years ago. Are labor-management relations better or worse now? Are wage demands forcing the companies to go under?
- Coal transportation depends on railroads. So, if the railroads are sick, could coal be well?
- Coal is black and sooty and gives off a lot of smoke. Surely this is an ecological menace. Who, if anyone, is paying attention to this prob-

lem? Or is it really a problem? Coal mining destroys the beauty, and probably the ecology, of the countryside. Is this really so? Might the Sierra Club have useful data on these questions?

- Perhaps coal is not sick, just bituminous coal. Maybe the anthracite industry is flourishing. Surely there is a trade association of coal-mining companies with data here. Call up the nearest big coal-mining company and find out its name and address from the public relations office.
- Perhaps coal is okay, but Wichahissic has a problem. But then again, Wichahissic does not seem to be as much in the news as Pokanoka, whose plight seems to be the archetype for "the depressed area." Check BLS (Bureau of Labor Statistics) for unemployment figures here.

Writing memos of this kind to yourself is useful not only at the beginning of a project but whenever you feel yourself beginning to drift toward panic or confusion. Following this initial stock-taking, you should think of yourself as designing, executing, and periodically read-justing a research strategy that will exploit certain predictable changes in your potential for gaining and utilizing information:

- *Locating relevant sources.* Over time, you decrease your uncertainty about what is worth knowing and how to learn it.
- *Gaining and maintaining access to sources.* (a) Over time, you aug-ment your capacity to obtain interviews from busy or hostile per-sons, and to obtain data that are not clearly in the public domain; (b) over time, you also—and unavoidably—use up your access to certain sources, and you must therefore conserve such exhaustible resources for use only when the time is propitious.
- *Accumulating background information as leverage.* Over time, you improve your capacity to interpret data and to force them out of reluctant sources, thereby increasing your background knowl-edge.
- *Protecting political credibility.* Over time, the research process itself creates an environment that will either help or hinder the adoption and implementation of your—or your client's—eventual recom-mendations.

The optimal strategy for managing any of these problems may conflict with the optimal strategies for dealing with the others. Each of these problems is discussed in a separate section, the final section of this chapter being reserved for a brief treatment of the trade-offs involved in trying to meet all strategic imperatives simultaneously. I assume throughout that the reader is an inexperienced policy researcher who has had academic training in the social sciences. Hence, I go to some lengths, at various points, to allude to differences between social science research methodology and the methods of policy research. I trust that the more experienced researcher will also find some profit in the arguments here, if only to conceptualize more clearly what she has already learned to do intuitively.

Another clarification about the intended audience is also in order. You start your task with certain resources and constraints, some of which are derived from your own experience and personality and others from your institutional location. Although institutional location is especially important in designing an optimal research strategy, it will not be discussed in this book. Suffice it to say that the resources and constraints of a legislative staff assistant are quite different from those of her counterpart in a bureaucratic setting and are even more dissimilar to those of a student working with a campus-based Public Interest Research Group (PIRG). The strategic advice offered here is intended to be sufficiently general to meet the needs of researchers in any of these circumstances, however.

LOCATING RELEVANT SOURCES

Unlike most social science research, most policy research is derivative rather than original. That is, it is produced by creative play with ideas and data already developed by others. Only occasionally does the policy researcher set out to generate his own data or assume responsibility for inventing a bright policy idea from scratch. His role is preeminently discovering, collating, interpreting, criticizing, and synthesizing ideas and data that others have developed already. To be sure, social science research often works this way too, but it also places a much higher premium on originality. In a sense, the policy researcher becomes an expert on experts—those scholars and persons of experience who are thought to be relatively sophisticated about the policy area.

Consulting Both Documents and People

In policy research, almost all likely sources of information, data, and ideas fall into two general types: documents and people. By "documents" I mean anything that has to be read: Web sites, journal articles, books, newspapers and magazines, government reports, statistical archives, interoffice memoranda, position papers, bulletins, and so on. By "people" I mean anyone, whether a single individual or a group, who is to be consulted in person. Research on any policy problem usually entails a canvass of both types of sources.

Avoid the pitfall of overemphasizing one type at the expense of the other. Sometimes one falls into the trap out of habit: if you start out interviewing experts, experienced administrators, and other informed persons, you continue doing so until you come to define "interviewing" as what your job is all about. You forget that the experts themselves typically have obtained a good deal of their expertise by studying documents, and that much of what administrators offer can also be found in agency reports, legislative hearings, published statutes and regulations, and so on.

Another reason for getting stuck in one medium and neglecting the other is an individual preference for less or more personal interaction, that is, for choosing to conduct your research via the Internet or in libraries (or files, in an organizational setting) or for concentrating on fieldwork instead. But it is usually desirable not only to consult both types of sources (documents and people) but also to consult them in alternating order: a spate of interviewing followed by a retreat to the Internet or the library followed by another round of interviewing, and so on. If for no other reason, there is probably a psychic economy in arranging and executing a fieldwork agenda in a consolidated time span, as there is in collecting and exploring a large body of documentary material.

In a more general way, however, it should be remembered that one source should be used to locate another and that this branching out can just as easily lead from one medium to the other as it can from source to source of the same type. More explicitly: people lead to documents as well as to other people, and documents lead to people as well as to other documents. There are thus four basic branches on the tree of knowledge, each of which I discuss in turn.

People leading to people.   Often one informant leads spontaneously to another by remarking during the course of an interview or conversation, "Have you seen X yet? She's very knowledgeable about . . ." This information can be stimulated by the researcher's asking questions such as "Who else would be a good person to talk to about . . ?" or the more specific "Who would be a good person to see in Agency Y?" For reasons of tact, one might frame the question more tentatively: "Do you think it would be advisable to talk to X—or do you think that would not be advisable?" Sometimes it is a good idea to ask the informant explicitly if his name can be used in seeking an appointment with the person he has suggested. This gives him an opportunity to protect himself if he does not want his name to be used and an opportunity to encourage name-dropping if he believes it will serve his interests. (That is, A may wish B to know that A has spoken of him as "a knowledgeable person" or words to that effect.) Make sure that the informant provides sufficient contact information for anyone he recommends seeing so that it is possible to locate the person.

Knowing whom to stay away from is often an important by-product of inquiries such as these. If the informant is trusting and wishes to be helpful, she may volunteer a cautionary aside such as, "If you do go to see X, you'll probably find him reserved if not unsympathetic." Unless X is a very important step in the developmental sequence at that moment, this might very well be a clue not to approach him until better groundwork has been laid for such a meeting. Another important by-product of such inquiries is a file of information on who is friendly, or antagonistic, to whom. Such information will be useful in constructing a map of political and administrative feasibility for any new program that you may eventually propose.

People leading to documents.   Just as one can ask informants whom else to see or talk to, one can also ask them what else to read and how to obtain it. In visiting informants in their offices, you can sometimes get useful hints by scanning the bookshelves and the papers on tables and desktops for titles and authors or agency names. Also, take all the documents away from the interview that the informant is willing to give you, even if you are not sure how relevant they are. The chances are good that you will turn up some interesting new material in the collection you eventually develop, and in any case, you may avoid a trip to the library should you later wish to quote them or to report precise bibliographical information. Finally, put yourself on mailing lists, so as to be on the receiving end of whatever stream of reports, bulletins, newsletters, circulars, and so on are distributed by organizations operating in the policy area. Many agencies keep budgetary and other numerical information in electronic spreadsheet form; ask if the files can be sent to you or, better yet, burn a CD with the files before you leave the office.

Documents leading to documents. Anyone who has ever written a substantial academic research paper in history or the social sciences has probably learned how to use one document to discover another through Web links, footnotes, and bibliographies. The same procedures work in policy research. In addition, one frequently uncovers references that are incomplete from a strictly academic point of view but that may still be useful for policy research. These are references to agencies or organizations (and even individuals) that have an ongoing responsibility for or interest in the policy area, and some of them can be expected to sponsor studies, reports, position papers, and so on that may prove invaluable.

Once research is under way, documents lead to documents in a relatively straightforward manner and without much difficulty. The problem is in knowing where to start when the research effort is just beginning. The easiest place to begin is the Internet, where it will probably not be difficult, using Google or some other search engine, to find the sites of advocacy groups putting forth their views of the problem and possible solutions. These sites probably contain valuable information and are a useful source of ideas and further leads. Because they are likely to be one-sided, however, you should try to find advocacy sites with opposed views.

But advocacy groups are just a beginning. More useful are the Web sites of policy think tanks, such as the Brookings Institution and the American Enterprise Institute (AEI). These are relatively mainstream institutions that produce a large number of policy-relevant papers annually in almost all policy domains. The best of the papers connect concepts from the social sciences (often by noted scholars) with applied problems. These papers will often provide an overview of some policy area. Brookings is sometimes said to be a "liberal" think tank and AEI "conservative." There is some truth in these characterizations, but it is not as important as the fact that both institutions care about their reputation for sound analytic work. One might fairly say they have political "orientations" rather than "biases." The same is generally true of the "liberal" Center on Budget and Policy Priorities, the "conservative" Heritage Foundation, and the "libertarian" Cato Institute. In the environmental area, the leading think tank is Resources for the Future, which favors a benefit-cost approach to environmental policy.

The Web sites of various governmental oversight institutions can be very helpful once you have in mind a particular legislative or regulatory issue. The Congressional Budget Office (www.cbo.gov) does hundreds of studies per year and posts many on line. The Government Accountability Office (www.gao.gov) does the same.

Do not be satisfied with only the sites that are accessible by means of a public-domain search engine. If you have access to the on-line resources of a university (or governmental) library, use it. University or governmentwide libraries typically subscribe to databases that can provide access to full-text newspaper and magazine articles (Lexis-Nexis), as well as abstracts and full-text publications in scholarly journals (JSTOR in particular). *The CQ Researcher Online,* published by CQ Press, provides access to feature-length journalistic articles dating back to 1991. *National Journal* is similar to *The CQ Researcher.*

Because Internet sources are so accessible, it is easy to forget about books (until the day they are all online, of course). Unfortunately, electronic search procedures do not work as well for finding good and appropriate books as they do for finding articles and relatively ephemeral materials. The best way is to find out what the experts and advocates recommend. You can check the bibliographies in journal articles or— following the "people leading to documents" strategy—ask them.

Documents leading to people.   Once having read, or read about, the work done by certain experts, academic or otherwise, you may wish to consult with them face-to-face or by telephone. You should be wary, however, of mistaking the nominal author of a study for the real one, particularly when she or he is a person or group in officialdom. The nominal authors of Supreme Court decisions, to take an extreme example, are the Associate Justices, but the real authors are usually their clerks, who in turn probably draw most of their arguments from the briefs filed by the lawyers on the case. Similarly, you should look behind the agency official whose name appears on the cover of a report, to locate the staff who did the work and may be named on the inside pages or referred to in a preface.

Seeking Secondhand Information

To find out what Senator A is doing or thinking about a policy problem, one need not necessarily ask the senator herself. Tens or hundreds of individuals may know the answer, or at least part of the answer. Such secondhand information must be used cautiously and constantly checked for bias or error. But it is not in any a priori sense inferior to information obtained firsthand, which may have its own biases and factual errors. To use a legal analogy, one relies for "truth" on witnesses rather than on the defendant, who after all cannot easily or prudently be asked to testify against himself. Sometimes it makes sense to obtain firsthand information as a supplement to the other, particularly if there is reason to think that failure to do so might ultimately jeopardize the credibility of the final research product.

The use of secondhand sources is especially important in seeking political feasibility data. Suppose, for example, that you are planning to recommend that emergency ambulance services be centralized under the city police department, and you want to estimate the probable reaction of the fire chief to such a recommendation. You could ask the fire chief himself, but he might not be willing to tell the truth, especially if he were going to hold out his acquiescence in return for better terms or for some reciprocal benefit. That is, he might in principle be willing to go along with the change—he might even be enthusiastic about it—but for bargaining purposes he might not be prepared to say so. On the other hand, he might really be against it but not willing to admit that because he thinks people might call him an obstructionist. In either case, the fire chief is not a reliable source of this information. Eventually it might be desirable to ask him his opinion directly, but one could probably learn as much or more by asking instead a variety of secondhand sources, such as a veteran city hall reporter, rank-and-file fire fighters, someone in the city manager's office, and someone from the police department.

Finding Multiple Sources of Firsthand Information

Suppose you wish to know about the past relationship between the police and fire departments. Have they been relatively cooperative, antagonistic, or indifferent? If for some reason you do not wish to ask the fire chief, it is always possible to ask the police chief, since she has also been a partner to these relations. Her view or interpretation of the relationship may differ from that of the fire chief, but she is as much a participant and her knowledge just as direct.

This principle has numerous applications. If you want to know what happened at a particular meeting to which you were denied admission (or to which you could not go for other reasons), there are many participants to query. If you want to know how one particular participant behaved at that meeting, you do not necessarily have to ask that participant. You can ask others who attended. If you wish to see a memorandum sent by Smith to Jones, you can ask either Smith or Jones, depending on which one you believe will be more agreeable—or you can obtain a photocopy from a third party.[1]

Searching for Sources and Searching for Knowledge

At the beginning of a policy research project, the researcher faces a dual uncertainty: about what she thinks she ought to know and about where

---

1. The notion of systematically using secondhand sources and the notion of finding multiple sources for firsthand information are foreign to the spirit and practice of much social science research, which typically assumes that when one wants to know the mental states or the conduct of a given individual, the best source is that individual. Such research then worries about how to devise measuring instruments and interviews that will register these facts about the individual with the least distortion. Often this is quite appropriate for the questions about which one does basic and original research, when the object is to get pure data for pure understanding. But in policy research, the problem is to get a sufficient understanding of the world to be able to make estimates about alternative courses of action. Since there is much uncertainty about the future, and so many uncontrollable variables that will enter into future action, too much precision about the past and present frequently gets in the way.

she can turn to learn it. These are interdependent questions, in the sense that the reduction of one type of uncertainty is both a consequence of and a condition for the reduction of the other.

Consider first what happens as the researcher clarifies her ideas about what she thinks she ought to know. Simultaneously, she is able to exclude certain sources she would otherwise have consulted and, because she knows better what her objectives are, she is able to intensify her search for sources of greater relevance. This is the classic research model, in which ends determine means—that is, a constantly evolving set of knowledge objectives gives shape to the strategy of source selection and consultation. It is as applicable to policy research as to any other sort of social inquiry.

Its exact opposite is also applicable. Because the cost of searching for adequate sources is so high in time and energy, when you find a rich source it is wise to mine it intensively, even if that decision slightly alters your original knowledge objectives. If you wish to make recommendations to the state legislature concerning the reduction of criminal recidivism rates, for instance, the most relevant data source (recidivism in that particular state) may not be as rich—and therefore useful—as data from the bureau of criminal statistics run by some state that does an especially good job of collecting such data.

One danger in this sort of pragmatism is that you will spend too much of your time on what appears to be a rich source, not knowing that there are much richer ones just around the corner. That is why it is wise to invest a good deal of time initially in canvassing a variety of possible sources and developing a broad overview of both the policy area and what means there are to learn about it. After this initial survey, it is possible to return to sources that look unusually rich. This procedure also guards against the second, and more important, danger in letting the sources guide you: you might lose sight of more desirable and feasible knowledge objectives. In the final analysis, there must be a balance between the classic model of ends (knowledge) dictating means (sources) and the pragmatic model of ends evolving out of the means one has at hand.

GAINING ACCESS AND ENGAGING ASSISTANCE

Gaining access can be a problem. If you wish to interview Assembly Member Jones, you must persuade Jones's appointments secretary that you are on serious business and that in any event you will not be put off. You must arrange an appointment for a not-too-distant date and persist even after Jones breaks the first appointment and fails to show up for the one made in lieu of that one. If you may wish to interview Jones a second time, you must take pains to keep this possibility open, and perhaps to foster it by your conduct during the first interview.

You may need to engage the active assistance of some informants, especially those who stand at the gateway to an agency's performance and budgetary data. Often these data are in a raw state—that is, the data are in the files but need to be collated and tabulated. Sometimes the data are in a semiprocessed condition; that is, they have been collated and tabulated, but they have not been put in a format intelligible to the researcher. (They are still in a format that is intelligible to the program managers, but this format does not fully reveal the meaning of the data to the researcher.) In such a case, you may wish to know about seeming inconsistencies in the classification of cases, or about the meaning of certain class designations that the managers have developed for their own decision making.

Finally, there are data that have been prepared for public use but that have not been processed completely or adequately for your purposes. Suppose the intramural evaluation staff of a state penal institution, for example, has issued its annual report on releases and recidivists, but you cannot tell from the report how reliably they have ascertained the prior arrest and conviction records of the so-called first offenders. Did they rely on probation officer reports? On prison records? Records from other states? The error structure of an agency's data is often not known to the agency, and if it is, it may not be made known to the public. In this case, as in the case of raw and semiprocessed data, interpretive assistance is needed from the agency itself. How much assistance it is willing to give may depend, in part at least, on how well you have established rapport with the agency and its personnel.

Getting an Appointment

Why should any informant grant you, a mere policy researcher, an interview? American manners and mores provide the most compelling reasons; it is part of our definition of courtesy. If someone talks to you, even through your appointments secretary, you are supposed to talk back. Of course, the more powerful, busy, or politically defensive the personage besought, the less will be the force of simple courtesy. In such cases, you might try to appeal to a sense of noblesse oblige or, if you have a prestigious institutional affiliation, to a willingness to exercise your caste privileges. In addition, many people simply feel flattered by the interest of an outsider—even a policy researcher—who wants to listen to them.

More reliable than these appeals to courtesy or vanity, however, is an appeal to political self-interest. Try to indicate that the outcome of your research is likely to have a bearing on the interviewee's (or her agency's) political fortunes and ambitions. It would therefore be prudent for her to be cooperative, to arrange for you to hear her (or her agency's) point of view, and indeed to use the interview setting to assess the relevant political implications of your work. Of course, it may require some fast talking over the telephone, when you call for an appointment, in order to set her mind thinking in these directions. In dealing with an appointments secretary, who will probably be even less sensitive to your political cues, you might have to make your points indelicately explicit. Instead of relying on the vagaries of a telephone conversation or an appointments secretary, it might be useful to write a letter requesting an interview, followed up by a telephone call.

Your informants will often be acquainted with one another and will occasionally talk among themselves about you and your work. Since you want such discussions to serve your interests rather than to work against them, you should try to develop a reputation as a competent, knowledgeable, and energetic researcher who is likely to produce something of intellectual or political significance. The best way to develop such a reputation is actually to be such a person, but in addition, certain stratagems may prove useful. Attempt, for instance, to become a familiar face, by attending meetings and conferences that your potential informants attend, and by loitering around office cafeterias or after-hours places that they frequent. Try to impress people with your ability to gain entree to meetings that are only quasi-public in nature, and by talking in public places to important personages. All this familiarity will backfire if you appear pesky or inept, so some judiciousness is in order. Also, you should appear to be learning quickly and critically while in these settings, rather than observing passively and dully. A notebook or laptop computer, in which you enter notes fast and furiously, is a good stage prop as well as useful in its own right. Likewise, animated conversation, preferably observed rather than overheard, can enhance your appearance in these settings. But do not be indiscreet by becoming a bearer of information from one interviewee to another.

Fieldwork does not proceed rapidly or smoothly. For the most part, you are a hostage to other people's schedules. You can expect delays of several days to several weeks between the time you request an appointment and the appointment date—and even longer if your informant eventually breaks the appointment and reschedules it for a few weeks later. (Sometimes it seems that research is mainly idle waiting!) This problem is particularly acute if delay in seeing one informant becomes a bottleneck to seeing others. To minimize idleness, it is a good idea to have two or three independent streams of interviewing running simultaneously, so that a bottleneck in any single stream cannot halt your work altogether.

Cultivating Access

Securing repeated access to an individual or agency presents different problems from securing a one-time-only appointment. Courtesy is of almost no use here; the political motive, conversely, is critical. Since the political impact of your work on certain individuals and organizations will almost certainly be adverse, some doors will inevitably be closed to you. Beyond a certain point, there is nothing to be done about them, except to seek alternative means of entry. A perceived political affinity helps, but not much. Repeated access depends, instead, on building personal rapport. This takes time, especially if you are not inclined to appear more friendly and congenial than you really feel. Rapport follows most of all from simple exposure. Think of yourself as an anthropologist who has to spend several months living among the tribe she is studying before being allowed to observe certain sacred rituals and practices.

At the risk of sounding patronizing, I will nevertheless note here that the research should observe the basic courtesies. Be on time. Dress appropriately, which generally means with the same degree of formality as the interviewee or just a little less. Be friendly without being overly familiar or presumptuous. If you tape interviews—always a good idea, in order to preserve a record—set up your equipment with minimal fuss and explain that the tapes are for your own reference only. State that you will turn off the tape whenever the informant wishes you to do so.[2]

Almost invariably, whoever actually assists you in collating and interpreting agency data will see himself as "doing you a favor," regardless of how insistent his superiors have been that he make his services freely and generously available to you. As part of the protocol for such a "favor," you must reciprocate with expressions of gratitude for his "going out of his way." An even more cooperative informant might mail you a copy of a speech she has recently given, knowing that it will be of interest to you. Or she might see to it that you are put on the list of invitees to a banquet at which you will be able to meet a number of potential informants in an informal setting. To a certain extent, this sort of assistance can be encouraged simply by letting people know that it will be welcomed. It can be facilitated by offering telephone and fax numbers or e-mail and postal addresses where you can be reached or where messages can be left for you. It may even be useful to have business cards printed with this information; relative to other research expenses, this one is quite small and can return high dividends.

Exhausting Access

Access can be exhausted, too, not just cultivated and built up. Whereas in some cases repeated exposure helps the researcher build rapport, in others exposure simply tears it down. In the extreme instance of the latter, one exposure is all the relationship will bear; this commonly occurs when the informant is defensive or antagonistic, or when he is extremely busy and cannot easily be imposed upon. Other instances are intermediate: the informant is willing to grant two but not three interviews—or three but not four. When you suspect that access to an informant may be exhausted relatively quickly, defer interviewing her until later in the research process, principally because your accumulated knowledge will then support a more productive interview.

---

2. If you come to sensitive material in the interview, remind the interviewee of your earlier offer to turn off the tape recorder.

Usually, deferring interviews with such informants inflicts no hardship on the researcher, since in the earliest stages, research can be conducted by talking with the legion of lower-level officials and administrative assistants, public relations officers, and so on. Potentially useful information sources are to be found in retired officials and in agency officials who are part of a dissident faction.[3] These are rich sources at any time, but they are especially valuable in the early stages of research when it seems advantageous to defer approaches to more highly placed figures in the political establishment.

The researcher's reputation is also susceptible to being exhausted. It is perhaps not in danger of being lost, strictly speaking, so much as it is vulnerable to being transformed into a liability. Instead of being thought of as fair-minded, discreet, intelligent, and self-possessed, one may begin to be regarded as a partisan, a tale-bearer, a dope, or a dupe. The best way to avoid acquiring such an undesirable reputation is to eschew partisanship and indiscretion and, as I have already indicated, to actually be intelligent and self-possessed.

CONDUCTING A POLICY RESEARCH INTERVIEW

Policy research, in its completed form, becomes a political resource. Whatever its merits or demerits as a piece of rational analysis, it amounts to more than that. It may become a justification for certain parties to attack others or to defend themselves against attack, hence a weapon of persuasion in a war of propaganda. Although the tone and format of published policy research are typically neutral and disinterested, everyone recognizes that the research may be and often is used for political purposes, either by the author or by others. Hence informants are highly sensitive to the political implications of whatever they tell you. How an informant treats you depends in large part on how she thinks your work will be brought to bear on her personal or political interests.

Being wary of the possible political implications of what they might reveal, informants may be reluctant to talk freely and honestly. You should

---

3. My former Goldman School colleague William Niskanen relates that colonels twice passed over for promotion to general were a favored source for civilian policy analysts like himself in the U.S. Defense Department.

assume that all interviewees confront this problem, even though you may not know to what degree. In more extreme cases, it may be necessary to use various subtle kinds of leverage against the interviewee. Before turning to the problem in its most severe forms, though, I will sketch a basic strategy for conducting policy research interviews in general.

Energizing and Steering the Conversation

The interview process is an interaction carried on between the informant and yourself. In this process the principal source of energy should be the informant. Your tasks are, first, to encourage the informant to talk and to keep on talking, and, once a suitable momentum has been attained, to steer, to redirect, to slow down, or to cross-examine.

In addition to the political motivation, informants will talk because they have a story to tell. It is safe to say that many politicians, administrators, and important staff feel (correctly) that much of their best and most valuable work, which is being done behind the scenes, is unnoticed and underappreciated. They will be surprisingly eager to use you as their conduit to the outside world. Some also want to make their "side of the story" better understood than they think it is—and, if you haven't heard it from others yet, you may be surprised at how interesting it is.

In most social science research involving interviews, it is assumed that the interviewer is, as much as possible, a neutral instrument for recording data emitted by the respondent. However, this is generally an inappropriate model for policy research interviews. Here the informant assumes that you as an interviewer are anything but a neutral instrument—and it would be foolish for you to try to appear in such an ill-fitting disguise—since the whole object of your research is to arrive at some policy recommendations. Thus, you need not fear to probe the informant with provocative and even argumentative questions or comments—or to answer questions in return. Such exchanges can cause an informant to sharpen her wits and tone up her memory, and they may raise her psychic metabolism sufficiently to infuse energy into the whole interview process. If this is done with proper finesse, the informant will appreciate the stimulation. Your finesse as an interviewer, of course, consists of being argumentative without sounding (or being) closed-minded or hostile. It is a good idea to introduce contentious remarks in such a way that the informant, should she wish to do so, can retreat gracefully from the matter at hand into another topic—thus keeping her energy level up rather than dropping into an embarrassed taciturnity.

Most interviews are conducted at the informant's place of work. Sometimes, however, a more informal setting, such as a restaurant or café, should be chosen. Your method of note-taking should be compatible with such an informal setting—perhaps on the back of an envelope handily stored in your pocket for just such occasions.

Apart from energizing the informant, your other main function in the interview process is to steer her onto topics of interest to you. How can this be done?

Sometimes you must interfere in the informant's conversation stream simply to reestablish your right to speak, temporarily slowing the informant down without making her lose too much momentum. This can be done by interrupting with a short string of easily answered factual questions pertaining to the subject matter she has been discussing. The content of these questions, or at least the last one in the string, should be such as to work a transition to the next topic you have in mind. Suppose, for example, that you are interviewing the integrated-social-services coordinator in your county and she is telling you about her agency's relations with the county's chief administrative officer (CAO). Having heard enough on this subject, you now want to steer her onto her agency's current budget request to the U.S. Department of Housing and Urban Development (HUD). The conversation might go like this:

INFORMANT: . . . so you see we've had a devil of a fight with the CAO all the way. Maybe it's not her fault, of course, the Board of Supervisors being so conservative and the CAO needing support for her reappointment . . .

RESEARCHER: [Interrupting] Yes, she is up for reappointment this year, isn't she?

INFORMANT: Yes.

RESEARCHER: Well at least she doesn't control your budget, does she?

INFORMANT: True enough.

RESEARCHER: But HUD does—and how are your relations with them? Do you get pretty much what you ask for from them, in the way of a budget, I mean?

The point is not to disguise from the informant the fact that you are trying to steer her away from one topic and onto another, although sometimes this is desirable and should be attempted. The point is really to help her move from one topic to another without having to lose momentum or to feel awkward. Indeed, she will sometimes feel trapped on a topic that she herself would prefer to leave, and your job at such moments is to help her maneuver off the subject. If you cannot think of where you wish to lead her next, just think of a subject that is not implausible and that is not too demanding emotionally or intellectually. While you go in slow motion through that topic, both you and the informant will have a chance to collect your thoughts and feelings preparatory to moving to the next matter of serious concern.

Involving an informant in discussions of personalities is a delicate matter. The informant must be reassured that you are not turning the interview into a gossip session, that she is not a purveyor of gossip, and that you are not a seeker of it. This can be done by first introducing the name of the personality in a neutral, usually factual, context:

RESEARCHER: A few moments ago you mentioned the Southside Community Health League. Dr. Green has been head of that for about a year now—or is it two?

INFORMANT: Probably closer to two.

RESEARCHER: Maybe it just seems shorter because I remember Dr. Black, his predecessor, so vividly.

INFORMANT: Yes, Black was quite a leader there.

RESEARCHER: Seems people have been more critical of Green—though I have heard quite complimentary things from some sources.

INFORMANT: Yes, he's pretty controversial. He's certainly a competent administrator and has been pretty nice to us—though we deal mainly with his deputy, Mr. White.

RESEARCHER: How come?

Thus the conversation is turned to personalities by a sequence of small steps, in which each participant encourages the other and in which both assume responsibility for whatever gossipy quality may eventually threaten to intrude. Since personalities are such a sensitive topic, it is even a good idea to sprinkle your conversation with allusions to people about whom you may have no desire to question the informant. When you do want to pursue a discussion of a particular personality, this procedure makes the discussion seem less of a departure from the normal course of topics.

If the informant has unpleasant things to say about the personality under discussion, you might take pains to establish your own social, personal, and political distance from that individual. In the example just given, for example, the researcher has referred to "Dr. Green" rather than "Bill Green" and has indicated his distance by suggesting that he is unfamiliar with certain particulars of Green's career. If the informant has flattering things to say about the individual in question, you might choose to follow a contrary course, though it is always a little risky to appear very close to anybody, lest it arouse suspicions of partiality.

Leveraging the Defensive Informant

Occasionally one encounters an informant who is irrevocably committed to a defensive posture, for whom "No comment" is the primary defense and calculated evasion is the fallback position. Try to diagnose this problem very early in the interview and then reassess your goals for the interview in light of it. Concentrate on gaining information about specific questions that this informant is able to answer but that are probably not answerable by any other source. Since so much of your energy will have to go into cracking the informant's defenses, focus on some very specific objectives and begin to probe for them right away.

Once these preliminary assessments are out of the way and the interview has turned to specifics, the use of leverage is in order. First, let the informant understand that you are aware of his defensive posture, and signal that you do not intend to be put off by it. You might try to communicate that his defensiveness will not help him, that you know too much already to be shunted aside, and that you have access to other sources who have already told you much and to still others who will be willing to tell you more. Indicate that information from these sources may be more prejudicial to his interests than his own revelations would be, and that he therefore has nothing to lose, and perhaps something to gain, by giving honest answers. A certain amount of bluffing may sometimes be necessary, though this tactic carries obvious risks. It is always better to actually know as much as you pretend to know, and to have access to the sources you claim to have access to, than merely to bluff. Here is a sample of such an interview, with the head of a prominent local insurance company whom the researcher is pressing hard:

RESEARCHER: One thing I'd like to get more information about is the problem insurance companies have writing policies for merchants in so-called ghetto areas.

INFORMANT: [Silence. Pause.]

RESEARCHER: I mean, there may be problems because these policies are risky business propositions.

INFORMANT: [Silence. Pause.]

RESEARCHER: People say they are risky, anyway. Do underwriters in this area consider them risky?

INFORMANT: I can't really say for sure.

RESEARCHER: Well, some people in the Black Merchants Association claim that insurance companies won't write policies for them at all, that they've been classed as "unacceptable risks."

INFORMANT: I don't really know—insurance writing is the science of risks, isn't it?

RESEARCHER: [Decides that informant will provide no information on insurance industry doctrines or practices in general, or on the local underwriters in particular. Guesses that informant will be unwilling to discuss the doctrines, or rules, applied by his own company, and that she should therefore concentrate solely on gathering information about the practices of informant's company.] Perhaps I can clarify my question by being more concrete. In your own Bedrock Casualty Company, are applicants ever turned down because they are thought to be unacceptable risks?

INFORMANT: I can't say for sure. I'm not that close to the operating details of our very large company.

RESEARCHER: Of course. [To signal she will not be put off] You, or perhaps your secretary, could arrange for me to talk to someone at that level, though, couldn't you? [Seeking a different leverage point] But tell me about the category of "unacceptable risks." Does Bedrock Casualty tell its salespeople that the company will insure any premises provided the insured pays a high enough premium? [Shifting the terms of the question to throw informant off guard] Or is there a limit on how high a premium the company will set?

INFORMANT: Well, we do not like to charge exorbitant premiums, of course . . .

RESEARCHER: [Interrupting] So within the existing limits on premiums there might in fact be businesses too risky to insure—hence "unacceptable"? [Holding to offensive] How about cancellations? Has Bedrock canceled or refused to renew any policies of ghetto merchants even though they have not filed any claims recently? This is another thing the Black Merchants Association has been complaining about.

INFORMANT: [Deciding researcher knows more than he had thought and deciding to get preemptive protection against the Black Merchants Association's allegations] Well, yes, we have canceled a few, in the more riot-prone areas, and refused to renew other policies in that area. We had no choice; we stood to lose a lot of money in case of any trouble.

RESEARCHER: [Graciously ignoring this "confession," and trying to induce informant to tell his side of the story] Of course, that's quite understandable. I think most people recognize this problem. [Now taking aim on a single statistic, the proportion of all Bedrock policies in ghetto neighborhoods canceled or not renewed in the last two years] In the past, have you written many policies in that area?

INFORMANT: Yes, we've done quite a bit, in the past anyway.

RESEARCHER: You still do insure some business over there, don't you?

INFORMANT: Yes, we do, though as I say, I'm not too close to the operating details . . .

RESEARCHER: [Interrupting] Could you estimate what proportion of your policy holders from, say, two years ago you continue to insure? Is it 80 percent, 20 percent? Just to give me some rough idea.

INFORMANT: Well, it would certainly be a lot closer to 80 than 20 but I really don't know.

RESEARCHER: [Deciding that this would be an interesting datum and that it is worth pursuing vigorously] Can we find out?

INFORMANT: Not easily. It's not in any files anywhere in that form, and it would be awfully difficult to find out.

RESEARCHER: [Not believing that it would be very difficult, deciding that she is willing to contribute her own labor to searching the files, if necessary, and resorting to a bluff] People have the impression that Bedrock is less inclined to write policies for ghetto merchants than other companies in this area. I don't know where the facts come from—but I think some lawyers connected with the Black Merchants Association have been looking into legal aspects . . .

INFORMANT: What? I'm sure we are no worse, or different, than any other company in town! I'd like to see these so-called facts!

RESEARCHER: If I get any further clarification on that, I'd be happy to let you know. Meanwhile, I'd be willing to help out in whatever way you like in getting this information together concerning your own company's record in this field.

Let us interrupt this scene without a conclusion because, however it turns out, the researcher has done the best she could. The president of Bedrock Casualty may deliver the sought-for information, or he may not. Good interviewing strategy and tactics do not guarantee success, especially when the odds are weighted against the researcher to begin with.[4]

---

4. The researcher's bluffing tactic in this scene is of debatable morality. Although I believe it would be unethical in most circumstances, there are occasions when it would be justified. This is one of them. In this case, the Bedrock president seeks to withhold proprietary information. Does he have a right to do so? Normally, yes. But this right has to be weighed against the injustice of depriving ghetto merchants of a nearly essential prerequisite for doing business when they might be perfectly willing to meet reasonable price terms for acquiring the insurance (perhaps with government or philanthropic assistance). The researcher here has an arguable right to try to combat this injustice. Given that right, does she also have the right to use deception? The use of explicit deception on the part of the researcher is balanced by the use of implicit (covert) deception on the part of the president.

One common ploy used by a defensive informant is to reel off masses of irrelevant statistics and facts, which can easily swamp a naively data-worshipping researcher. Another ploy is to ramble garrulously about side issues, while running out the clock on whatever time limit he has set for the interview. Your best defense against these evasive tactics is to be able to recognize them for what they are.

If your own leverage fails—and if the elusive information is sufficiently important to you—you may be able to use someone else's. A graduate student researcher may have little leverage with determinedly defensive bureaucrats, for instance, but a legislator, or her staff assistant, will almost certainly have more. Hence, as a last resort, the student might persuade a sympathetic legislator to help out. Sometimes a newspaper reporter or an established group can be of assistance. The local medical society, for example, might be able to get information from the county hospital administrator about hospital policies that no academic researcher—and perhaps not even a county supervisor—could get.

A significant constraint on using leverage is the desirability of maintaining cordial relations with whatever agency or individual is being pressured, for the researcher runs a clear risk of alienating the objects of his leveraging tactics. With respect to a given study, this problem can be mitigated by postponing the more offensive tactics until relatively late, when the study is less vulnerable to being undermined by the offended party. The problem is more difficult, however, when the researcher envisions a long-term relationship—lasting well beyond the conclusion of the present research effort—with the agency or individual under scrutiny. Certain information may have to be sacrificed in order to preserve a modicum of goodwill for the future.

USING LANGUAGE TO CHARACTERIZE
AND CALIBRATE

The basic medium of the interview is spoken language embedded in a conversational context. Such a medium, when used as a representational device, presents reliability and validity issues (in psychometric terms).

The simplest issue—to see, though not necessarily to resolve—involves the language of characterization. If an informant says, "Yes, this is a frustrating job," you have to interpret both the nature and intensity of the word *frustrating,* and do so in a way that permits you to calibrate the result against some larger frame or benchmark. This can be done by asking a series of questions designed to do the calibrating. One shortcut is to start by offering up your own characterization and see how the informant reacts to it: "If I had this job, I would find it awfully frustrating, I think." This quickly establishes a benchmark of some kind— "awfully frustrating"—for you and the informant to use. Of course, there is the problem of knowing whether you and your informant mean the same thing by the expression, since your frustration thresholds may differ. But you're off to a good start.

An improvement on the last example would be to create two such benchmarks, that is, to describe a whole continuum with anchors at both ends, and perhaps a verbal midpoint. For example: "Would you say that your reaction to proposal X was extremely skeptical—as I've inferred from what you already have said—or was it relatively favorable . . . or was it maybe 'wait-and-see'?" This sort of approach has the added advantage of respecting virtually any position your informant holds and of communicating your willingness to find anchoring words based in the informant's own history. Or you could anchor one or both ends in what "other people" have supposedly been saying.

To be sure, by characterizing the available options in this way you are putting words into other people's heads and sometimes into their mouths. Before you proposed "extremely skeptical," your informant might never have thought of the proposal in this way, and now you run the risk that by asking the question you have created such a thought out of thin air. But that comes from using language as a medium. It can't be avoided. Even when you use the ostensibly neutral and clinical language that survey researchers and reporters use, you are putting words into people's heads and mouths. My more provocative characterizations, when used as benchmarks, are on a logical par with the more neutral alternatives offered by survey instruments and professional journalists.

PROTECTING CREDIBILITY

Like social science research, policy research is eventually subject to criticism on intellectual grounds. But unlike social science research, it is even more vulnerable on political grounds and, indeed, is vulnerable to attack by the very subjects of the study. In social science research, the subjects rarely become significant critics of the product, but in policy research their criticism is inevitable. Therefore, the researcher should take steps to protect the ultimate political credibility of his work from politically motivated as well as strictly intellectual attack.

Defending against Politically Inspired Criticism

In contrast to social science research, the primary goal of policy research is not intellectual enlightenment (either of the researcher or of her professional colleagues), although enlightenment is inevitably a by-product. Instead, the goal is to improve one's understanding of a policy problem, and of possible means of coping with it, to the point at which it becomes possible to advocate a responsible course of action. Thus, policy research takes aim at broad and complex phenomena, and so it is typically satisfied with very gross approximations of "truth," in contrast to social science research, which typically seeks more refined interpretations of narrowly circumscribed problems. The gross and approximate character of policy research is an open invitation to politically inspired criticism. How can the researcher protect herself?

For one thing, she should attempt to touch base with any party (or any institutional interest) who might later try to undermine the report by claiming to have been ignored. Indeed, it is a good idea to preempt such claims by quoting the party in the report, as evidence of a sort that the party's views were taken into account. For instance, if the researcher is going to recommend alterations in the way superintendents are selected in a given school district, it would be best to interview representatives from the local association of school administrators and from the local chapters of the National Education Association and the American Federation of Teachers. Spokespersons for these groups may have interesting opinions to contribute to the research project, but even if they do not, by consulting them the researcher gains protection against their criticisms should they decide to oppose the recommendations in her report. It may even be useful to send out a preliminary copy of the report to these interests for reviews.

Second, the researcher should seek out "experts" or others with political or intellectual authority to whom to attribute views, opinions, estimates, and so on, about which she feels especially uncertain. Quoting published sources is one way of making such attributions, and including quotations from interviews is another. In addition, the researcher should line up experts who will be willing to speak up in support of her work once it becomes public. Sources who are quoted in the report as having a view on this or that become natural targets for inquiring journalists or political decision makers; these sources have an incentive to defend their quoted views when questioned.

Third, the researcher should pay special attention to potential opponents and identify which propositions they are likely to attack. These target points should be bolstered in advance by expert quotations, and some polite reference should be made to the existence of counterarguments—without at the same time giving them too much space or prominence. The very opponents who can be expected to raise objections later should be quoted, in order to defuse any claims that their arguments or positions were ignored. (There may be additional psychological advantages to the balanced or two-sided presentation, simply as a subtly persuasive form of propagenda directed at the reader.)

Statistics can be useful for buttressing credibility. Employed for this purpose, they play a documentary rather than an informational role. Statistics can document the validity of generalizations that political opponents might otherwise challenge, even though their truth is abundantly evident through more impressionistic sources.

Preparing for Premature Exposure

Politicians and policy researchers work on different timetables. The former often call for "results" well before the research is in any sense finished. Even when no one demands it, however, unexpected opportunities often do present themselves before the researcher's work is close enough to being finished that he could seize the auspicious moment to present his results.

One possible strategy is to map out (as much as possible) the timetable of potential political demands and to arrange your research timetable in at least partial correspondence. Another strategy is to prepare yourself as soon as possible with answers to the crudest kinds of questions that might be asked of you. Since these are generally the kinds of answers politicians need and want anyway, you may as well formulate them early in the course of your research. Finally, it is important, early on, to line up your supporting experts, as well as to touch base with potential opponents. Since, once again, these contacts must be made eventually, there is good reason to make them sooner rather than later.

STRATEGIC DILEMMAS OF POLICY RESEARCH

By way of summary and conclusion, let us consider the question: Which informants should be approached when? Answering this question forces a useful review of most of the issues discussed earlier.

We may divide the "when" part of the question into "relatively early" and "relatively late" in the course of the research project. Approach the following informants relatively early:

- Persons who are likely to facilitate your search for rich information sources
- Powerful persons who directly or by your reputed connection with them will facilitate your access to sources
- Knowledgeable persons who will provide you with the information you need to hedge against premature political exposure of your work, and whose information will contribute to your capacity to exert leverage against defensive interviewees
- Friendly experts who will contribute to your political credibility in case of premature political exposure
- Potential opponents with whom you touch base in order to hedge against premature political exposure

Approach these informants relatively late:

- Hostile or defensive informants against whose tactics a prior buildup of leverage is desirable
- Busy informants to whom you might lose access permanently once you have seen them, or about whom you are not sufficiently informed to interview early
- Potential opponents, especially if powerful, who might try to forestall your access to others and thereby cripple your research efforts

- Administrators who have knowledge of potential trouble spots but who will be unwilling to point them out until it appears to be in their self-interest

There is one obvious contradiction between these two lists—approach potential opponents early and late—and several others that are not quite so obvious. Often it is the busy and the defensive informants who are also in the best position to facilitate the search for sources, open doors, and provide useful information. Top agency administrators, for instance, may have plentiful experience with the policy problem under investigation and can provide easy access to sources, but they also have a vested interest in maintaining the status quo or something very close to it. In any event, they may not take kindly to having their activities scrutinized too carefully by an outsider. Other similar examples can easily be called to mind. There is in principle no way to reconcile these incompatible prescriptions of whom to approach early and whom late. You will have to consider the full details of your particular situation and then balance the risks and rewards inherent in any given choice. There is no way of avoiding such trade-offs; you should simply make them consciously rather than inadvertently.

"SMART (BEST) PRACTICES" RESEARCH: UNDERSTANDING AND MAKING USE OF WHAT LOOK LIKE GOOD IDEAS FROM SOMEWHERE ELSE

I t is only sensible to see what kinds of solutions have been tried in other jurisdictions, agencies, or locales. One looks for those that appear to have worked pretty well, tries to understand exactly how and why they might have worked, and evaluates their applicability to one's own situation.[1] In many circles this process is known as "best practices research." Simple and commonsensical as this process sounds, it presents many methodological and practical pitfalls. Part III helps you avoid the pitfalls and offers tips on how get the most pay-off from your search for best practices.

DEVELOP REALISTIC EXPECTATIONS

First, don't be misled by the word *best* in best practices research. Rarely will you have any confidence that some helpful-looking practice is actually the best among all those that are addressed to the same problem or opportunity. The extensive and careful research needed to document a claim of "best" will almost never have been done. Usually, you will be looking for what, more modestly, might be called "good practices."

But even this claim may be too grand. Often you can't even be sure that what appears to be a good practice is actually good in the sense that it is solving or ameliorating the problem to which it is nominally

---

1. Readers interested in a more social scientific exposition of many of the points in Part III should consult Bardach 2004.

addressed. On closer inspection, it may turn out that a supposedly good practice is not solving the problem at all. Inadequate measurement, plus someone's rose-colored glasses, was simply producing the illusion of mitigating the problem. It may also turn out that, even if good effects have truly occurred, the allegedly good practice had little or nothing to do with producing them. Finally, innocently extrapolating from a setting where a good practice has indeed worked well to settings that differ in little-understood but important ways could lead to weak, perverse, or otherwise damaging results.

None of these problems is decisive, though. If it does nothing else, a foray into "best practices research" usually turns up interesting ideas, including ideas about what does *not* work as well as what does.

ANALYZE "SMART PRACTICES"

A "practice" is a tangible and visible behavior. When you can ask someone what their practice is in addressing some problem, they can answer with a description of what they do. Typically, though, a practice is also an expression of some underlying idea—an idea about how the actions entailed by the practice work to solve a problem or achieve a goal. Some such ideas are particularly "clever," and I shall explain further what I mean by this. The practices that embody them I call "smart practices."

Finding the Free Lunches

One way of being clever is getting something for nothing. Contrary to the dictum that there is no such thing as a free lunch, creative policymakers and policy implementers invest quite a lot of energy in looking for just such comestibles. Often, they are successful. To understand how this can be, consider the free lunch cornucopia produced by the natural sciences and engineering. The energy stored in the chemical bonds in a cup of gasoline can run a car for a few miles provided one knows how to access that energy and channel it. Pulleys and levers supply mechanical advantage. Bacteria happily eat and destroy the organic crud in a city's wastewater almost for free. All these materials, devices, and conditions amount to getting a lot of "something" for nothing or for relatively little. The source of all these boons is simply Mother Nature.

In the social world, the sources of something for nothing are usually less tangible and less directly gifts of Mother Nature, but they are no less real. The "invisible hand" of the market creates social value where only individual pursuit of self-interest had once been, and, metaphorically at least, it operates without charge. Alphabetical ordering permits people to find information in a fraction of the time it would have taken had there been no such ordering. Queuing at bus stops is easy to understand and usually fair, and it makes life better for everybody.

In the world of policy and management there are no doubt fewer and less delectable free (or nearly-free) lunches than in the marketplace or in some information storage facility or at a bus stop, but they are there. All the "opportunities" described in Box I-1 (p. 8) have this latent potential to generate something of public value relatively cheaply. (On the nature of "public value," see Moore 1996.) One might say that the difference between the (high) value created and the (low) cost, and risk, of producing it represents a free lunch.[2]

Opportunities don't deliver up their latent value without some additional work, however. This work is done by the practices that take advantage of their potentialities, and these typically cost something and are subject to various vulnerabilities as well. However, the smarter these practices are, the more value they can manage to extract at lower cost and risk.

The following list contains some examples of candidates for smart practice status—candidates, that is, because to my knowledge they have not all been subjected to the extensive empirical testing needed to confirm such status:

- A "high-expectations" welfare-to-work program. Implemented in the early 1990s, the Greater Avenues to Independence (GAIN) program I studied in Riverside County, California, was a prototype for the 1996 federal welfare reform act. Unlike most other welfare-to-work programs, the Riverside program set high expectations about work for GAIN participants in two senses. In many different ways, it

---

2. Risks come in several varieties; see the section called "Describe Generic Vulnerabilities."

signaled participants that program staff had confidence in (high expectations of) their ultimate success in getting a job and getting off welfare. This confidence was intended as an antidote to the low self-esteem, and consequent low effort to reattach themselves to the labor force, of many participants. Staff also signaled—and expressed in program rules about early and diligent job search, as well as through a variety of formal and informal pressures—that "society expected" welfare participants to shape up and take responsibility for their own financial well-being. The Riverside GAIN program designed its recruitment, training, performance appraisal, and other administrative systems to support this high-expectations philosophy (Bardach 1997). In effect, the high-expectations model took advantage of the natural energies to solve their own problems that program managers assumed to be latent in the program participants.

- *Reading One-to-One.* A tutoring program for children in Grades 1–3 who have fallen badly behind in learning to read English was created by George Farkas of the social sciences faculty of the University of Texas at Arlington; it was first tried out in Dallas and then spread to Houston and a number of other cities. The program involves systematic instruction in phonemic awareness, one-to-one tutoring by a well-trained tutor, and highly structured feedback and supervision. Like all phonemics-based programs, it recognizes that English orthography does not map sounds in a systematic or logical way and that it is at some point necessary for learners to master the decoding and encoding rules actually in use. It takes advantage of the fact that children's early failures in reading that come from neglect of phonemic awareness are reversible by regular tutoring. It also takes advantage of the emotional bonding that comes with the one-to-one tutoring relationship. The simplicity and systematization of the teaching materials, teaching methods, and administrative oversight system make the program easily replicable and keep the costs relatively low (Farkas 1998).

- *Sharing maintenance responsibilities for a neighborhood park between the local parks department and the residents of the neighborhood.* Nonprofit organizations often spring up to provide services of a nonstandard sort not provided by the public agency (e.g., same-sex schools, abortion clinics). An extension of the basic idea is a partnership in which the public sector supplies certain resources that are not only supplementary but also complementary. In many a city, the city government provides the parkland and the neighbors provide some or all of the labor to make the land more serviceable in some way. This practice takes advantage of two interesting potentialities: the potential for gains from trade between two parties, and the use of what is in effect barter, in a situation where there are administrative and political barriers to organizing the transaction in cash.

- *The "expenditure control" budget.* Adopted first in the city of Fairfield, California, this practice was publicized by David Osborne and Ted Gaebler (1992) in their influential book, *Reinventing Government.* As originally conceived and implemented, this budgeting strategy gave each department the same basic mission and the same budget as in the previous year (with an inflation adjustment) but abolished the line-item specification of expenditures, permitting the department to keep any savings and reinvest them in other mission-related activities. This approach took advantage of the superior technical and operational knowledge of program implementers relative to that of elected officials and bureaucrats in fiscal-control agencies.

- *Milestone payments to nonprofit service contractors.* In 1992 the Oklahoma Department of Rehabilitation Services began paying nonprofit contractors for the rehabilitation milestones, defined in performance terms, that mental health clients could achieve en route to higher levels of employability.[3] The clients got to participate in assessing whether the milestones had been met, while vendors got to help the department define generic milestones and other aspects of the program. The milestone system also permitted contractors to claim reimbursement from the state on a more

---

3. This program was a 1997 finalist in the Ford Foundation/Kennedy School of Government (KSG) Innovations in American Government competition. My source for information about it was the Innovations program files.

accelerated schedule than they had previously been able to do, thereby taking advantage of the power of self-interest to motivate better performance from the nonprofits. It also provided greater transparency than more traditional fee-for-service arrangements, under which the funding agency did not know much about the quality of the service provided.

- *A cooperative project between rehabilitation and recycling programs.* Hennepin County, Minnesota, arranged for mentally retarded clients of the county vocational rehabilitation program to sort and recycle discarded auto batteries, an item of concern to the county's environmental management agency.[4] The two programs thus took advantage of production complementarities between physical and human "assets" that they could deploy.

Note that I have made a point, in describing each of these supposedly smart practices, of saying that the practice "takes advantage" of something. This is a linguistic device for ensuring that in analyzing how the practice "works," we make sure to focus on those aspects of its "works" that are central, that is, on the fact that the practice aims to exploit or take advantage of, some latent opportunity for creating value on the cheap.

Breaking Loose from Conventions and Assumptions

Another way of being clever is not so much technical—finding those free lunches—as ideological and psychological. It involves disrespecting conventional boundaries. In the world of public policy and management, this sometimes involves challenging assumptions anchored in value commitments. For example, since the late 1980s we have begun to shake loose the assumption that just because some good or service is "good for the community" and ought to be *financed* through taxation, it ought also to be *produced or delivered* by governmental employees. Instead, we now can contemplate contracting out to the nonprofit or even the profit-seeking sectors such traditionally "governmental" functions as primary education, correctional institution construction and

---

4. This was a Ford/KSG semifinalist. See Borins 1998, 200; also, I had personal communication with Hennepin County program managers.

management, and welfare-to-work programming.[5] In this case, we are challenging the assumption that governmental provision necessarily embodies a social expression of the value of community. Taxpayer financing might do so, but governmental provision does not.

Another value-oriented smart practice might simply be to articulate the values that underlie a program and make it effective. Riverside's high-expectations welfare-to-work model, for instance, was one of relatively few programs prior to the mid-1990s that decided it was proper to articulate the value premises that underlay its approach to case management.

OBSERVE THE "PRACTICE"

In free-lunch-type situations, we can say the smart practice is "whatever takes advantage of—or exploits—the latent opportunity to create value on the cheap." [6] But let us try to say more about how to characterize this "whatever."

Characterizing the Features of a Smart Practice

The basic mechanism in a smart practice is how it directly accomplishes useful work in a cost-effective manner. A smart practice is made up of (1) the latent potential for creating value (from Box I-1, for instance), plus (2) the mechanism for extracting and focusing that potential. In the six examples described earlier, I indicated the basic mechanisms by saying what each of the practices "takes advantage of." For instance, the shared maintenance for parks takes advantage of potential gains from trade and the opportunity to use barter as substitute for cash payment.

But there is more to a smart practice than this basic mechanism (Bardach 2004). Some characteristic secondary features of a smart practice are the following:

- *Implementing features,* which directly implement the basic mechanism. In the Oklahoma milestones case, for instance, they are the

---

5. Whether or not contracting out is a smart practice, it is highly controversial, I might add.
6. With minor adjustments the same analysis can also be applied to "practices" whose "smartness" derives from their departure from convention.

payment schedule, payment amounts, and payment conditions. In the Hennepin County recycling/rehabilitation program they are the stock of recyclable materials, the pool of mental retardation clients, and the interagency understandings that link them.

- *Supportive features,* which are primarily those resources used to bring the implementing features into being—for instance, a budget and an institutional structure. Other supportive features that have a less directly instrumental role but may nevertheless be important might include the culture of the organization or the broader political environment.
- *Optional features,* or those that just happen to be of interest to actors in the site where the practice is observed but may not necessarily be valued elsewhere. For instance, in the Oklahoma milestones case, the feature that allows vendors to participate in the design of the program seems to me optional—although nice!

Distinguishing Functions and Features

In adapting a seeming smart practice from a "source site" for application at a "target site," you want to be rigorous in replicating the logic—the "how"—of the basic mechanism, while leaving maximum flexibility as to the specific means to carry it out. To do this, distinguish between the *functions* involved in getting the mechanism to work and the particular *features* that embody those functions. For instance, in the milestones program, the functions include setting the milestones and verifying the claims of achievement. These actions are part of the defining logic of the practice—they cannot be omitted without changing the very essence of the program. However, exactly what features are chosen to implement these functions or to support the implementation strategy is another matter. With regard to the high-expectations welfare-to-work program, two essential functions are creating a moral climate favoring responsibility and instilling self-confidence that such responsibility can be met. Exactly what design features should be chosen to implement and support these functions is more open-ended, though.

Here is a linguistic hint to help you separate features and functions: Functions should be formulated as gerunds, verb-like nouns ending in "ing"—as I did above with *setting, verifying, creating,* and *instilling*—

while the features that perform these functions can be indicated by pure nouns.

An exception to this principle of formulating functional language arises when you really need or want to specify a particular method for carrying out a function. In the milestones case, for instance, you might intentionally refer to a contract as a specific means of defining expectations among the parties and to documents as a means of attesting that the milestones have been met.

Allowing for Variation and Complexity

Because smart practices are internally complex, context-sensitive, and can be used by different parties to pursue slightly different bundles of goals, how we talk about them should reflect these qualities.

Characterization should be generic and flexible, not prescriptive and overly precise.   Consider the expenditure control budget described earlier. Does the practice there require giving *all* the savings back to the department, or would, say, 50 percent qualify? If the basic idea is to provide incentives to spend wisely, returning 50 percent might suffice. Probably the best characterization, therefore, would be "allowing the department to retain *enough* of the savings for its staff to feel motivated to create the savings in the first place." [7] It would then be up to whoever implements the expenditure control budget to determine what "enough" means in the local context.

I would also say that it *should* be left to local implementers to figure out the details of the generic practice that make sense in their own context. Allowing for local adaptation of nonessential features not only serves common sense but also encourages greater buy-in by the locals to a practice that in some sense is being imported from elsewhere or, worse yet, imposed from outside.

Characterization of the basic mechanism of a smart practice is not necessarily simple; it could be complex.   In my list of examples of candi-

---

7. Note that this is an interpretation asserted by the researcher-observer, not necessarily something that has actually been done in practice or endorsed by any practitioners.

date smart practices, I included only relatively simple practices, so as not to cause confusion. However, some smart practices are multifaceted, complex, and not easy to summarize in a few sentences or even paragraphs. Michael Barzelay analyzed what he called the "postbureaucratic paradigm" for managing statewide overhead and control functions in Minnesota state government. He considered trying to reduce the many aspects of this postbureaucratic paradigm—which I would also call a smart practice, albeit a very large practice—to a few "core ideas" such as "service," "customer focus," "quality," "incentives," "creating value," and "empowerment." However, he concluded, "the major concepts . . . are not organized hierarchically, with one master idea at the top," but are instead arrayed as "an extended family of ideas" (Barzelay 1992, 115–117).

A related management reform paradigm, called by many the "new public management" (NPM), emerged in New Zealand in the mid-1980s as another such "extended family" of ideas and practices. Noting that it "is not reducible to a few sentences, let alone a slogan," one observer goes on to state its "key ideas," as follows:

- Government should provide high-quality services that citizens value.
- The autonomy of public managers, particularly from central agency controls, should be increased.
- Organizations and individuals should be evaluated and rewarded on the basis of how well they meet demanding performance targets.
- Managers must be assured that the human and technological resources they need to perform well will be available to them.
- Public sector managers must appreciate the value of competition and maintain an open-minded attitude about which services belong in the private, rather than public, sector. (Borins 1998, 9)

Specimens of a smart practice in the real world look rather different from one another and require careful interpretation. You should try to find multiple exemplars or specimens of a smart practice to get a sense of its robustness and efficacy when (1) it is being implemented under different supportive (or antagonistic) conditions, (2) it comes with different optional features attached, and (3) it employs supposedly equivalent but nevertheless somewhat different means to perform the required functions. Ideally, you would be able to find social scientific evaluation studies of practices that would supply both data and theoretical interpretation regarding such matters. In most cases, however, such evaluations will not exist. Normally—or perhaps at best—you will find writings or speeches by practitioners describing successes in a few places, accompanied by only sketchy descriptions of what was done or the difficulties of implementation. You will need to think very hard and reason very carefully about how you will want to conceptualize (that is, define) the smart practice of interest and to assess the support requirements you think are the most important. You need to do this even before you get to thinking about how the practice might work in the particular context(s) you have in mind (see the later discussion of this point under "But Will It Work Here?").

DESCRIBE GENERIC VULNERABILITIES

It should be part of standard professional practice in describing smart practices to explain not only how and why they work but also how and why they fail, collapse, backfire, and generally make people sorry they ever tried them. That is, we should be told the nature of their *generic vulnerabilities*. A generic vulnerability is a potential weakness of the practice that is somehow connected with its basic causal structure. It may have to do with a high sensitivity to small errors in execution, or with the environment in which the practice is being implemented (e.g., an environment that might impose certain insupportable stresses).

Of course, all political and implementation environments are stressful to a certain degree, and we can reasonably include in the definition of a particular smart practice those features necessary to safeguard it against the more predictable and potentially damaging stresses. Without such safeguards, an otherwise smart practice could become a very dumb practice. For instance, although privatizing certain municipal service functions is a smart practice when would-be private suppliers operate in a competitive market, it might become a very dumb practice under these circumstances: (1) if it were to be carried out in an environment monopolized by a single supplier; (2) if the bidding process were very corruptible, and corrupt interests were to discover this fact; (3) if inappropriate performance measures were to be stipulated in the contract; or (4) if the municipal contract management procedures were overly rigid or overly lax. To take another example, a high-expectations welfare-to-work program is vulnerable to the condition of the local labor market: if unemployment is high and jobs are scarce, high expectations may produce in participants more defeatism about themselves and more cynicism about the "responsibility" that society is urging on them. A government/neighborhood "partnership" for park maintenance is, in a generic sense, vulnerable to, among other things, temptations on the part of policymakers to slowly shift more and more of the burden onto the neighbors while reallocating budgetary funds to other departments.

Generic vulnerabilities are only the *potential* for trouble, it should be remembered. Whether the troubles actually materialize depends on the nature of the local environment in which the smart practice is implemented and on the success of various parties who are aware of the vulnerabilities in designing and implementing successful countermeasures. Contracting processes, for instance, can be designed to minimize corruption, albeit at some cost. And neighbors entering into a partnership with the city regarding parks maintenance might insist on putting the terms of the partnership in writing and holding a well-photographed press conference to announce them. Even if such a document had no legal standing, it would give neighborhood representatives some useful political leverage in later years.

Two particular types of vulnerability are especially worth attending to. One pertains to likely failures of general management capacity—such as a low general level of leadership talent or the lack of a "good government" ethos that would make it easier to implement this or any other practice successfully. The other pertains to weaknesses intrinsic to the particular practice itself—such as a service delivery program's susceptibility to conflict over whether to give priority to this or that catchment area or needy subpopulation, or a safety-oriented regulatory program's inability to determine whether to err on the side of injury-tolerant leniency or costly stringency.

BUT WILL IT WORK HERE?

Assuming that you have understood the essence of the generic smart practice very well, including its generic vulnerabilities, and have mapped the variety of supportive features that could increase its odds of success, in the end, you must still ask: "Assuming this practice is indeed smart in some contexts, is ours a context in which it can work well enough to warrant trying it?" Answering this question intelligently entails looking at both the source contexts, where the practice appears to have worked well, and at your own target context, where it is being considered for adoption.

Assessing the Target Context

Within your target context, a careful assessment of the present situation is in order, of course, but a static answer based on this assessment is not enough. You need to think also about what might be done at reasonable cost or risk to improve the prospects of the smart practice in the target context, were it to be implemented there. These actions fall into the following two categories:

- *Safeguarding strategies.* Consider the generic vulnerabilities of the smart practice: are the most dangerous of them likely to cause unacceptable trouble in your context? For instance, if excessive rigidity in the contract management process is a generic vulnerability of partnering with a nonprofit agency, are your contract management institutions known to be unusually rigid? And if so, is there anything you can do to offset this problem? Might you, for instance, find someone in the contract management bureau who can serve as a special protector and expediter? Or if you cannot do that, can you find some way to structure the contract terms so that the contractor is held accountable for achieving general results rather than for following specific procedures?
- *Enhancement strategies.* Consider what I called earlier the "supportive features" that can help a practice work better: What supportive features will be put into play? How well are they likely to perform? Can you do anything to improve them? For instance, can you attract top-notch personnel to manage this program or undertake this project? Can you obtain more stable funding than annual appropriations? Can you mobilize the press to take positive notice of what you are doing? Can you count on the support of key stake-

holders and relevant political constituencies—or at least on weak action from opponents?

Evaluating the Source Contexts

If you have to search very hard for smart practices that might be usable in your own situation, the chances are that the practice will not be very widespread. This means that the specimens you locate will come from jurisdictions, agencies, or locales where policymakers and administrators tend to look more favorably on novelty and innovation than is usually the case. Hence, their overall managerial capacity may be better than average, and perhaps better than the one in your own locale.

If the source contexts are largely pilot or demonstration programs, you need to be particularly cautious, because (1) pilot program implementers probably bring more enthusiasm and talent to bear on their work than the average program implementers, and enthusiasm and talent count for something; (2) the political and financial conditions at the pilot sites are probably more favorable (or less unfavorable) than those at the average site; and (3) bureaucratic resistance to a pilot is typically less intense than to a permanent change that threatens existing values, status, job security, or work routines.

How cautious should you be in extrapolating from successes observed in pilot or demonstration contexts? No systematic research exists to answer this question. However, a RAND Corporation analysis of a variety of juvenile crime prevention programs discounted the effectiveness levels attained in the pilot contexts by 15 to 40 percent when estimating a "scaling up penalty" that would apply when implementing the programs on a wide scale (Greenwood et al. 1995). Although the RAND analysts offered no explicit reasoning for choosing the penalty factors that they did, their choices do seem reasonable.

If you are analyzing the possibility of implementing a smart practice not just in some known local context but on a wide scale, you should be concerned about more than the fact that pilot program results may be much better than average. You should also be concerned about the existence of many *below-average* sites where the smart practice would be implemented—some of them perhaps quite a bit below average. In an era when it was much less common than it is today to think about the federal devolution of program and policy responsibilities to state governments, federal policymakers—particularly political liberals—often worried about the "Mississippi problem." Mississippi was the rhetorical symbol of the poor, backward, and probably racist jurisdiction that would almost surely wreck or pervert any smart practice it was given responsibility for implementing.

BACK TO THE EIGHTFOLD PATH

Given the typical shortfall of good evidence relative to theory and speculation when it comes to assessing a smart practice, there is a danger of unwarranted optimism. Indeed, a common criticism of the best practices research tradition is that it becomes excessively enthusiastic about what appear to be good ideas before their worth is sufficiently tested.[8]

But how much testing is "sufficient," anyway? The answer has to be framed partly in terms of the costs of displacing what might actually be a better practice, perhaps even the practices currently in use (described earlier as "letting present trends continue"). However, if one is reasonably confident that current practices are ineffective or harmful, the costs of wrongly abandoning them in favor of the new and untried may not be so high after all. Thus, although the new and untried should bear *some* burden of proof, it should not be an excessive one. The correct approach is to treat the risks and uncertainties involved in adopting some seemingly smart practice as comparable to the uncertainties associated with all the other alternatives under consideration.

Of course, the costs of change—negotiation, insecurity, hard feelings, and so on—must also be counted against bringing in a new and seemingly smart practice. But such costs must be counted against any change, not just change to accommodate smart practice. Moreover, if institutions and people are very stuck in their ways, there may be benefits to change as such, not merely costs.[9]

---

8. Unfortunately, excessive enthusiasm for experiments that eventually fail gives even appropriate enthusiasm for experimentation a bad name.

9. Alternatively, if institutions and people are forever being reformed and reinvented and remodeled—as occurs in many public school systems—there may be benefits to stability, consistency, and focus

SPECIMEN OF A REAL-WORLD POLICY ANALYSIS

The following text is excerpted from the policy brief "Mandatory Minimum Drug Sentences: Throwing Away the Key or the Taxpayers' Money?" prepared by the RAND Corporation. It is provided as an example of a policy document and was chosen for its thorough and focused analysis as well as its concise presentation. My annotations appear in the numbered notes below the text. The notes of the authors of the brief are indicated by asterisks.

PREFACE

In response to public concern over disparity of sentencing by judges and brevity of terms served by criminals, state legislatures and the Congress have written into law minimum sentences for specific crimes. In this report, we estimate the cost-effectiveness of mandatory minimum sentences for crimes related to cocaine distribution. These estimates are made relative to the cost-effectiveness of spending additional resources on enforcement without mandatory minimums and on drug treatment.[1]

Source: Jonathan P. Caulkins, C. Peter Rydell, William L. Schwabe, and James Chiesa, "Mandatory Minimum Drug Sentences: Throwing Away the Key or the Taxpayers' Money?" (Santa Monica, Calif.: RAND Corporation, 1997).

1. Cost-effectiveness analysis requires comparison. Often we compare the cost-effectiveness of some new state of the world with the existing state. But in this case they compare several alternative new states of the world.

Our central effectiveness measure is reduction of the nation's cocaine consumption, although we also examine reduction of cocaine-related crimes, along with decrease in cocaine spending, which is related to such crimes.[2]

Because this report may be read by people with diverse interests, it is divided into two parts.[3] Readers interested principally in narcotics-control and criminal-justice policy may wish to stop at the end of Part I. Part II has been prepared mainly for those also interested in the role and techniques of mathematical modeling in policy analysis, although some effort has been devoted to make it understandable to those not expert in this area.

This research was supported by a gift from Richard B. Wolf of Richland Mills and by funding from The Ford Foundation. This study was carried out within RAND's Drug Policy Research Center. The center's work is supported by The Ford Foundation, other foundations, government agencies, corporations, and individuals. It carries out extensive assessments of drug problems at local and national levels. Those interested in further information should contact the center at RAND's Santa Monica address.

SUMMARY

In recent decades, the American public has responded favorably to political leaders and candidates who have espoused longer sentences for the possession and sale of drugs. Among the more popular sentencing extensions are "mandatory minimums," which require that a judge impose a sentence of at least a specified length if certain criteria are met. For example, federal law requires that a person convicted of possessing half a kilogram or more of cocaine powder be sentenced to at least five years in prison.

Mandatory minimums have enjoyed strong bipartisan support from elected representatives and presidential candidates.[4] To these propo-

---

2. These different "measures" are our "criteria." Note that by making one "central" and two others obviously less so, the authors implicitly are differentially weighting the criteria.

3. They are "telling the story" to two different audiences—which amounts to telling two different, though related, stories. Presumably the authors could have issued separate reports, but the chosen format keeps complementary analyses together.

4. An important step in telling the story: establishing key features in the political environment.

nents, the certainty and severity of mandatory minimums make them better able to achieve incarceration's goals than are more flexible sentencing policies.[5] Those goals include punishing the convicted and keeping them from committing more crimes for some period of time, as well as deterring others not in prison from committing similar crimes. Critics, however, worry that mandatory minimums foreclose discretionary judgment where it may most be needed, and they fear mandatory minimums result in instances of unjust punishment.[6]

These are all important considerations, but mandatory minimums associated with drug crimes may also be viewed as a means of achieving the nation's drug control objectives. As such, how do they compare with other means? Do they contribute to the central objective—decreasing the nation's drug consumption and related consequences[7]—at a cost that compares favorably with other approaches? In this report, we estimate how successful mandatory minimum sentences are, relative to other control strategies, at reducing drug consumption, drug-related crime, and the total flow of revenue through the cocaine market. The latter is a worthy objective in itself—America would be better off if money spent on drugs were spent on almost anything else—and it is also associated with drug-related crime.

We focus on cocaine, which many view as the most problematic drug in America today.[8] We take two approaches to mathematically modeling[9] the market for cocaine and arrive at the same basic conclusion:

---

5. The proponents are projecting outcomes. The authors of this report imply that they do not necessarily accept these projections and that this analysis will do its own.

6. Proponents and critics clearly do not weight the evaluative criteria the same way. The authors imply that they hardly even notice one another's criteria.

7. Establishes "drug consumption" as the critical numerator in the cost-effectiveness analysis, though with others to be considered as well.

8. Narrowing the focus keeps the analysis manageable. The authors must justify the way they choose to narrow the focus, however. The shorthand version here is to call it "the most problematic drug," though without specifying what that means.

9. Not all models are mathematical. The phenomenon being analyzed here is complex, and formal modeling is both possible and desirable. Deciding on the values for particular parameters, such as the price elasticity of demand for cocaine, the cost to dealers of being caught, and the effectiveness of treatment, to name just a few, is somewhat speculative. The authors will use what evidence can be found in the research literature, however.

Mandatory minimum sentences are not justifiable on the basis of cost-effectiveness at reducing cocaine consumption, cocaine expenditures, or drug-related crime.[10] Mandatory minimums reduce cocaine consumption less per million taxpayer dollars spent than does spending the same amount on enforcement under the previous sentencing regime.[11] And either type of incarceration approach reduces drug consumption *less* than does putting heavy users through treatment programs, per million dollars spent. Similar results are obtained if the objective is to reduce spending on cocaine or cocaine-related crime.[12] A principal reason for these findings is the high cost of incarceration. (Note these findings are limited to relative cost-effectiveness. As mentioned above, mandatory minimums have been justified—and criticized—on other grounds.)

Reducing Consumption: More Enforcement against Typical Dealers

First, we estimate the cost-effectiveness of additional expenditures on enforcement against the average drug offender apprehended in the United States (whether that apprehension is by federal, state, or local authorities). In this approach, we track the flows of users among light-use, heavy-use, and no-use categories, and we analyze how overall cocaine market demand and supply respond to price. That is, if more money is spent on enforcement and incarceration, costs to dealers are increased, and so is the street price of cocaine; higher prices mean lower consumption.[13] If more money is spent on treatment, consumption is reduced for most clients while they are in the program, and, for some, after they get out. We estimate the changes in total cocaine consumption over time for an additional million dollars invested in the alternatives

---

10. The headline comes about as quickly as it possibly can. In italics, too.

11. Establishes "million taxpayers' dollars spent" as the critical denominator in the cost-effectiveness equation.

12. No matter which criterion is chosen, it just so happens that treatment turns out to be a better investment than tougher incarceration procedures.

13. Note the use of market theory to lay bare the heart of "the drug problem." You do not often see a newspaper account of "the drug problem" that refers to price movements, demand, and supply. Yet the "laws" of supply and demand apply, in some sense, to drug markets as much as they do to the market for green beans. It is almost impossible to project the effects of alternative antidrug interventions without taking into account how the market mediates whatever is done.

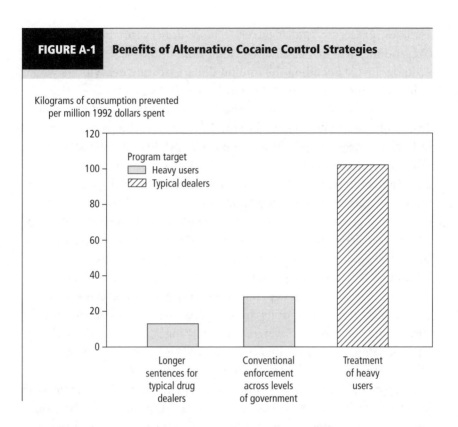

FIGURE A-1   **Benefits of Alternative Cocaine Control Strategies**

Kilograms of consumption prevented
per million 1992 dollars spent

Program target
☐ Heavy users
▨ Typical dealers

Longer sentences for typical drug dealers | Conventional enforcement across levels of government | Treatment of heavy users

considered. These changes, discounted to present value, are shown in Figure A-1.

The first two bars in the figure show the results of spending a million 1992 dollars* on additional enforcement by agencies at various levels of government against a representative sample of drug dealers. As shown by the first bar, if that money were used to extend to federal mandatory minimum lengths the sentences of dealers who would have been arrested anyway, U.S. cocaine consumption would be reduced by almost 13 kilograms. If, however, the money were used to arrest, confiscate the

---

* All cost calculations in this report are in 1992 dollars. The choice of a reference year for cost figures is arbitrary. We choose 1992 to facilitate comparison with the results of earlier analyses. To convert costs in 1992 dollars to costs in 1996 dollars (the latest year for which inflation data are available), multiply by 1.119. To convert kilograms of cocaine consumption reduced per million 1992 dollars spent to kilograms reduced per million 1996 dollars spent, divide by 1.119.

assets of, prosecute, and incarcerate *more* dealers (for prison terms of conventional length), cocaine consumption would be reduced by over 27 kilograms.[14] Spending the million dollars treating heavy users would reduce cocaine consumption by a little over 100 kilograms.

Note we are estimating the impact of an *additional* million dollars. The results can be extrapolated to multiples thereof, but not to extremely large changes in spending. They certainly do not suggest that the most cost-effective approach is to shift all drug control resources from enforcement to treatment. Note also that we refer in the figure to "longer sentences" rather than to "mandatory minimums." [15] Data on drug dealers arrested at state and local levels are insufficient to isolate those associated with drug amounts sufficient to trigger mandatory minimums. Instead, we analyze a hypothetical policy of applying the mandatory minimum sanction—longer sentences—to all convicted dealers.[16]

The values shown are dependent, of course, on various assumptions we make. If the assumptions are changed, the values change. But for changes in assumptions over reasonable ranges, do the values change enough to make longer sentences more cost-effective than either of the other alternatives? We find they do not.

As an example, the values shown are dependent on the time horizon in which one is interested. The reason for this is as follows. When faced with extended sentences, drug dealers will want more income today to compensate them for the risk of increased prison time. As a result, cocaine prices will go up and consumption will go down. Benefits from

---

14. Note the importance of defining "the margin" where the policy operates. The policy is twice as effective if you can restrict "the margin" to dealers who would not have been arrested anyway.

15. The political rhetoric might oversimplify by talking about "tougher" approaches to dealing, but the authors here distinguish two different forms of "tougher." Even more forms exist, of course.

16. All policies that deal with the future are "hypothetical." Why do the authors go out of their way to use this term explicitly here? Probably because they wish to distinguish the alternative they are analyzing from empirical specimens existing in the real world. They are more interested in a "generic" strategy based on mandatory minimum sanctions, a sort of composite of what does exist and what might exist in a more ideal form.

reduced consumption will thus accrue immediately, while the costs of the extended prison terms will stretch out into the future. In contrast, if more users are treated this year, the costs accrue immediately, while the benefits in terms of reduced consumption by those who stay off cocaine stretch out into the future. Figure A-1 takes account of these different allocations of costs and benefits across future years in that future costs and benefits are discounted annually, out to 15 years—a time horizon typical in analyzing public policy. Beyond that point, any further costs and benefits count as zero. What if that terminal point were moved closer? What if one had not just a discounted interest in anything beyond the immediate future, but no interest? If the time horizon is set early enough, the effect is to "zero out" both the future stream of costs from mandatory minimums and the future benefits from treatment. Figure A-2 shows the relative cost-effectiveness of the three programs analyzed when time horizons are set at various points, from 1 to 15 years. At 15 years, the lines match the heights of the bars in Figure A-1. The time horizon must be reduced to only about three years before mandatory minimums look preferable to additional conventional enforcement, and close to two years before they look preferable to treatment. Hence, mandatory minimums appear cost-effective only to the highly myopic.[17]

We also analyzed the implications of changing other assumptions. For example, dealers would want to be compensated for the increased risk of imprisonment they would incur in the event of increased enforcement. But the typical person would demand less compensation for being imprisoned five years from now than next year, and we assume drug dealers are even more "present-oriented." What would happen, though, if dealers wanted more risk compensation, and if they discounted future costs less heavily than we assume? Longer sentences would seem more burdensome than we assume, dealers would demand a higher premium for handling cocaine, the price of cocaine would rise even more with increased enforcement spending, and consumption would fall even

---

17. A bit of wit and rhetoric! Who says you have to be dry and boring in telling your story? The authors can get away with it here because their result is extremely robust—and because they are well-known and respected analysts in this field.

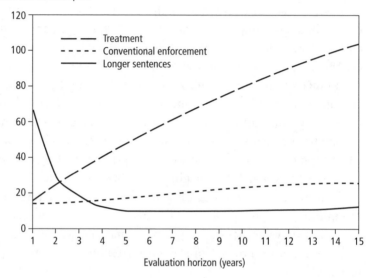

FIGURE A-2   Benefits of Alternative Cocaine Control Strategies for Different Time Horizons

Kilograms of consumption prevented per million 1992 dollars spent

Treatment
Conventional enforcement
Longer sentences

Evaluation horizon (years)

more. Consumption would also fall more than we expected if users were more responsive to price increases, i.e., if demand were more "elastic." We attempted to swing the balance toward extended incarceration by simultaneously increasing risk compensation by one-third, cutting the dealer discount rate by two-thirds, and increasing the elasticity of demand by 50 percent.[18] The general profile of our results did indeed change. The cost-effectiveness of longer sentences tripled, while that of additional conventional enforcement doubled, and that of treatment rose by about a quarter. However, longer sentences remained the least cost-effective alternative, and treatment the most.

18. This is another version of "sensitivity analysis."

Reducing Consumption: More Enforcement
against Higher-Level Dealers

The first two bars in Figure A-1 represent enforcement approaches applied to a representative sample of all drug dealers arrested. Perhaps mandatory minimum sentences would be more cost-effective if they were restricted to somewhat higher-level dealers. By "higher-level dealers," we mean those who operate at higher levels of the drug distribution system, who make more money and thus have more to lose from more intensive enforcement. To approximate such a restriction, we limit the set of offenders analyzed to those who are prosecuted at the federal level and possess enough drugs to trigger a federal mandatory minimum sentence.

The results are shown in Figure A-3. There, the darkest bars represent the reduction in cocaine consumption from spending an additional million dollars in enforcement against the federal-level offenders just defined. The light bars are those from Figure A-1. Reading from the left, each light/dark pair of bars represents the same kind of program. The distribution of long sentences is the same for the first two bars, and the kinds of additional enforcement actions funded (arrest, seizure, prosecution, and incarceration for conventional sentence lengths) are the same for the next two bars.

As shown by the darker bars in Figure A-3, the consumption change achieved per million dollars spent on mandatory minimums is closer proportionately to that achieved through the other alternatives. While longer sentences for a representative set of all dealers have 46 percent of the effect of additional conventional enforcement against such dealers, federal mandatory minimums have 57 percent of the effect of additional conventional enforcement at the federal level.[19] And, obviously, federal mandatory minimums do better relative to treating heavy users than do longer sentences for all dealers. To the higher-level dealers considered in this analysis, time in prison carries a greater cost, and amounts of cocaine and other assets seized through increased enforcement are also larger.

19. These percentages are calculated from numbers to be read off Figure A-3. One might wish the authors had somehow warned the reader that these numbers cannot be read off what is actually drawn in A-3.

FIGURE A-3 **Benefits of Alternative Cocaine Control Strategies**

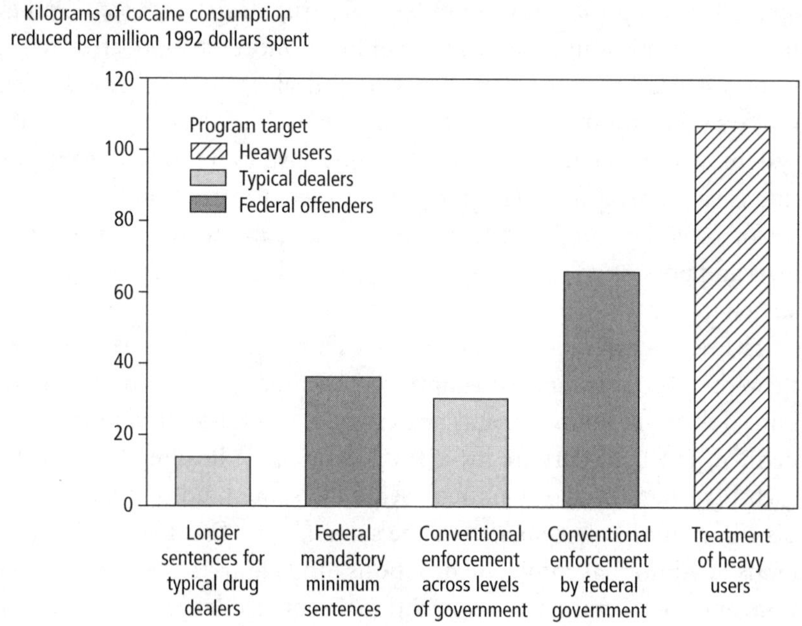

Kilograms of cocaine consumption
reduced per million 1992 dollars spent

Program target
- Heavy users
- Typical dealers
- Federal offenders

(Categories along horizontal axis: Longer sentences for typical drug dealers; Federal mandatory minimum sentences; Conventional enforcement across levels of government; Conventional enforcement by federal government; Treatment of heavy users)

Thus, risk compensation must be higher, and the higher resulting cocaine prices drive down consumption more. Nonetheless, at any given level of government, or against any given type of dealer, mandatory minimums are less cost-effective than conventional enforcement.

Why is that the case?[20] Drug enforcement comprises two types of components, each of which is costly for taxpayers and each of which contributes to keeping drugs expensive: (1) arrest and conviction, which impose costs on suppliers principally through the seizure of drugs and other assets, and (2) incarceration of convicted defendants. Amid complaints about the "revolving door" of justice, some overlook that arrest

---

20. Nice use of rhetorical question to vary the pace and tone.

and conviction impose costs on dealers. In fact, on average, arrest and conviction impose greater costs on dealers per taxpayer dollar spent than does incarcerating dealers. Since mandatory minimums alter the mix of these two components of enforcement in favor of incarceration, they dilute or reduce the efficiency of enforcement relative to simply expanding both components proportionately.

As with the light bars, the precise heights of the dark bars in Figure A-3 depend on various assumptions. Again, these include assumptions about such uncertain values as the compensation dealers would demand for increased imprisonment risk, the rate at which dealers discount future costs, the responsiveness of buyers to shifts in cocaine prices, what it costs to arrest a dealer, and the value of drugs and other assets seized. To test the sensitivity of our results to these assumptions, we vary the assumed values of factors such as these one at a time over substantial ranges. In all cases, conventional enforcement is more cost-effective than mandatory minimums, and treatment is more than twice as cost-effective as mandatory minimums. Even when assumed values are varied two at a time, large departures from assumed values are required for mandatory minimums to be the most cost-effective approach. In Figure A-4, for example, the government's cost of arresting a dealer and the compensation a dealer wants for risking a year of imprisonment are varied simultaneously. The star shows the values assumed for the results in Figure A-3. As Figure A-4 shows, mandatory minimums would be the most cost-effective alternative only if arrest costs were to exceed $30,000 and a dealer were to value his time at some $250,000 or more per year. Such dollar values would typify only those dealers at a fairly high level in the cocaine trade and who are unusually difficult to arrest.** For dealers costing less to arrest, cocaine control dollars would be better spent on further conventional enforcement. For dealers demanding less risk

---

** Even for these dealers, it is possible that conventional enforcement would be more cost-effective than mandatory minimums. That would be the case if the range of conventional sentences could be matched to the range of offenders so that the highest-level dealers received very long sentences.

compensation, the money would be better spent treating heavy users than on enforcement against such dealers.[21]

Long sentences could thus be a smart strategy if selectively applied. Unfortunately, because mandatory minimum sentences are triggered by quantity possessed and because those thresholds are low, they are not selectively applied to high-level dealers. (Indeed, anecdotal evidence suggests that high-level dealers can sometimes avoid mandatory minimums more easily than their subordinates. High-level dealers have more knowledge about their organization to use as bargaining chips with prosecutors. Furthermore, such dealers often do not physically possess their drugs, as is required for a mandatory minimum to take effect; they hire others to incur that risk. To the extent that this occurs, mandatory minimum sentences would be even less effective than these results suggest.)

Reducing Cocaine-Related Crime

Of course, cocaine consumption is not the only measure of interest. Many Americans are worried about the crime associated with cocaine production, distribution, and use. Using data on the causes of drug-related crime and our cocaine market analysis, we quantify the approximate crime reduction benefits of the various alternatives. We find no difference between conventional enforcement and mandatory minimums in relation to property crime; the former, however, should reduce crimes against persons by about 70 percent more than the latter. But treatment should reduce serious crimes (against persons as well as property) the most per million dollars spent—on the order of 15 times as much as the incarceration alternatives would.

---

21. The uninitiated reader needs more help in interpreting Figure A-4 than the authors provide. The figure is divided into three regions. Each region contains combinations of values for the two parameters "cost to government" and "cost to dealers." The boundaries between the regions indicate where the parameter combinations imply different winners in the cost-effectiveness competition that the authors have set up. Thus, mandatory minimum sentences win only when the parameter combinations fall in approximately the northeast quadrant, that is, when the costs are high both to dealers and the government. In other RAND publications, this sort of mapping is called "threshold analysis." I call it, in Part I above, "break-even analysis."

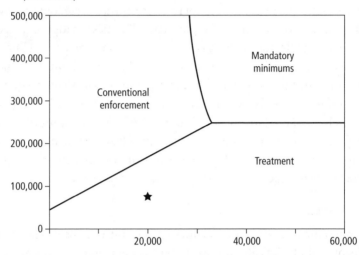

FIGURE A-4 **Which Program Is More Cost-Effective at Reducing Cocaine Consumption Under Different Assumptions?**

Cost to dealers per year of imprisonment (1992 dollars)

Mandatory minimums

Conventional enforcement

Treatment

Cost to government of making an arrest (1992 dollars)

Note: Star indicates values assumed for dark bars (federal offenders) in Figure A-1.

Why do we get these results?[22] Most drug-related crime is economically motivated—for example, undertaken to procure money to support a habit or to settle scores between rival dealers. Fewer crimes are the direct result of drug consumption—crimes committed "under the influence." However, we find very little difference between conventional enforcement and mandatory minimums in their effects on the money flowing through the market, and thus very little difference in their effects on economically motivated crime. We do find, as shown in Figure A-3, appreciable differences in consumption effects, and thus appreciable differences in effects on crimes committed under the influence. The latter are more likely than are economically motivated crimes to be crimes against persons.

22. Another well-placed rhetorical question.

Treatment, however, has an enormous advantage over enforcement in reducing the economic value of the cocaine market—larger even than that shown in Figure A-3 for reducing cocaine consumption. Why is that?[23] When a treated offender stays off drugs, that means less money flowing into the market. But when a dealer facing the risk of a longer sentence raises his price, say one percent, to compensate, buyers will reduce the amount of cocaine they purchase. The best evidence suggests that reduction will be something on the order of one percent.[24] Thus, the total revenue flowing through the cocaine market stays about the same, and so do the incentives for economically motivated drug-related crimes. Therefore, the effect of the enforcement alternatives is limited almost entirely to the relatively small number of crimes committed under the influence. Treatment, however, has an advantage against those crimes similar to that shown in Figure A-3 and an even greater advantage against the larger number of economically motivated crimes.

Conclusion

Long sentences for serious crimes have intuitive appeal. They respond to deeply held beliefs about punishment for evil actions, and in many cases they ensure that, by removing a criminal from the streets, further crimes that would have been committed will not be. But in the case of black-market crimes like drug dealing, a jailed supplier is often replaced by another supplier if demand remains. And not all agree whether mandatory minimums satisfy American standards of fairness and justice. Even those who believe they do must ask themselves to what extent might it be desirable to give up some punishment of the guilty to gain some further reduction in cocaine consumption—consumption that can victimize the

---

23. And yet another!

24. So they base their model's parameter estimates on some sort of evidence after all! Because this report "Summary" is a summary of the *logic* of their analysis, the authors do not trouble the reader with the details of how these projections were made, that is, how their model is constructed and its parameters assigned numerical values. These will appear in the full report. The word *evidence* here perhaps is intended to reassure the reader that, while the analysis herein is "hypothetical," as the authors indicated above, the hypotheses are to the extent possible based on a body of accumulated evidence.

innocent.[25] This trade of punishment for drug use reduction must be considered because long sentences are expensive and cocaine control resources are limited. As we show, if reducing consumption or violence is the goal, more can be achieved by spending additional money arresting, prosecuting, and sentencing dealers to standard prison terms than by spending it sentencing (fewer) dealers to longer, mandatory terms. (And that is to say nothing of what might be achieved by redirecting resources from enforcement to treatment—admittedly, a more difficult reallocation because those programs might be run by completely different agencies.) We find an exception in the case of the highest-level dealers—those who value their time most highly and are hardest to apprehend—where sentences of mandatory minimum length appear to be the most cost-effective approach. However, current mandatory minimum laws are not focused on those dealers.

---

25. The authors confront readers with a starkly defined trade-off.

APPENDIX

B

THINGS GOVERNMENTS DO

The following list of things governments do is meant to stimulate creativity and give you ideas. The way to use it is to think about your policy problem and then go down the list, asking yourself, "Might there be any way to use this approach on this problem?"

The "Why You Might Do It" discussion that accompanies each list of "What You Might Do" is necessarily brief. It is intended principally to be suggestive.

I. TAXES

A. What You Might Do

1. Add a new tax
2. Abolish an old tax
3. Change the tax rate
4. Change the tax base
5. Improve collection machinery
6. Tax an externality

B. Why You Might Do It

The most common conditions to which taxes are a solution are when there is inadequate government revenue for some purpose and—probably more important—when the structure of market prices fails to capture the true economic opportunity costs. If market prices are wrong, there are usually deeper structural reasons, such as oligopolistic power or government overregulation of some input, which might bear correcting by other means as well.

Naturally, too many taxes can also be a problem. They may be inhibiting useful economic or social activity.

II. REGULATION

A. What You Might Do

1. Add a new regulatory regime or abolish an old one
2. Write new standards or remove old ones
3. Tighten or loosen existing standards
4. Ban or prohibit something entirely
5. Improve the scientific and technical basis for writing standards
6. Close or open loopholes
7. Add, train, or better supervise enforcement personnel
8. Improve targeting of enforcement to catch bad apples, or to increase deterrence, or to increase resource efficiency
9. Raise or lower the level of effective sanctions
10. Tighten or loosen appeals procedures
11. Change reporting and auditing procedures
12. Add, subtract, or improve complaint mechanisms for workers or the public

B. Why You Might Do It

Distinguish three quite different types of regulation. One aims at prices and outputs in natural monopolies. The public utilities commission regulating local telephone service is an example.

A second type—sometimes called "social regulation"—is common in regard to health and safety issues. It aims to correct imperfections arising from poor market information or from excessive frictions resulting from the use of civil law (usually tort or contract) remedies. Drug safety regulation by the FDA is an example. Two sorts of problems are common in this type of regulation: too little regulation and too much. Scientific uncertainties, technical difficulties of measurement, and political pressures typically lead to both of these problems under varying conditions.

A third type of regulation concerns entry, exit, output, price, and service levels in supposedly oligopolistic industries (e.g., transportation).

Administering this type of regulation presents large problems of information collection and of coordinating the outputs of many firms. Politically there are often problems of anticompetitive "capture." The deregulation movement that has gathered political momentum since around 1978 has led to a new appreciation of how much beneficial competition there might be in these industries if government were simply to let go.

Most air and water pollution regulation is thought of as social regulation. However, administratively (and sometimes politically), it is more like the third type of regulation, inasmuch as the principal laws now on the books involve government agencies in coordinating the outputs of a variety of firms.

III. SUBSIDIES AND GRANTS

A. What You Might Do

1. Add a new one
2. Abolish an old one
3. Change the level
4. Change the marginal rate
5. Introduce, abolish, or change a formula by which subsidies are allocated
6. Modify the conditions of receipt or eligibility
7. Loosen enforcement
8. Tighten enforcement

B. Why You Might Do It

Incentive effects.   Subsidies and grants are often used to stimulate activities that neither markets nor nonprofit nor voluntary action appears to produce in adequate quantity or quality. They also play important roles in the system of intergovernmental relationships—when one level of government wishes to encourage another level of government to do certain things—and in the system of relationships between governments and nonprofit organizations.

Wealth effects.   Grants and subsidies also transfer resources to people or organizations or levels of government in order to make the recipients wealthier.

Some design problems.   It often happens that you want to create incentive effects but not wealth effects, or vice versa. For instance, you might wish to make poor people wealthier via grants and subsidies but without diminishing work incentives. Or you might wish to encourage businesses or universities to undertake more research and development of a certain kind but without unduly enriching them or allowing them to use the subsidies inefficiently.

Note that subsidies and grants are typically administered with various guidelines or conditions attached. The threat to remove a long-time grant or subsidy for violation of the guidelines or conditions can act as a type of regulatory sanction, thus making certain grants and subsidies into a peculiar regulatory hybrid.

IV. SERVICE PROVISION

A. What You Might Do

1. Add a new service
2. Expand an existing service
3. Organize outreach to potential beneficiaries not now using the service
4. Better customize an existing service to a particular subpopulation
5. Provide vouchers for a particular service so people may choose from an array of competitive service providers
6. Link two or more existing service delivery systems to take advantage of potential synergies or to make life easier for service recipients
7. Reduce service users' difficulties in accessing the service by
    a. going online
    b. computerizing intake and eligibility processes
    c. simplifying forms
    d. colocating services
    e. permitting appointments by phone
    f. facilitating personal inquiries and complaints
    g. improving payment options

B. Why You Might Do It

Services come in two basic flavors. *Desired services* are those people want, such as parks and good schools. *Paternalistic services* are those that people might or might not want but that outsiders want them to have because there is some potential payoff to the outsiders (e.g., rehabilitative services for the mentally ill, organized shelters for the homeless, job search services for individuals on welfare). It is a lot easier to design a service provision system for desired services than to do so for paternalistic services.

V. AGENCY BUDGETS

A. What You Might Do

1. Add a lot to the budget
2. Add just a little to the budget
3. Hold the budget at last year's level
4. Cut the budget a little
5. Cut the budget a lot—to the point of beginning to terminate the agency
6. Shift allocations from one budget item to another

B. Why You Might Do It

You might want to adjust an agency's budget according to whether you like what it does. In addition, how you manipulate an agency's budget sends political signals about the degree of satisfaction or dissatisfaction with the agency's performance and so may be thought to have incentive effects as well as wealth effects. It is not easy to use the budget as a means of creating incentive effects, however.

VI. INFORMATION

A. What You Might Do

1. Require disclosure
2. Direct government rating or certification
3. Standardize display or format
4. Simplify information
5. Subsidize production of information
6. Subsidize dissemination of information

B. Why You Might Do It

Information production, dissemination, and validation may be suboptimal due to the declining average (and sometimes marginal) cost nature of the activity. Information consumption may be suboptimal due to the hidden costs of consumption (such as time spent reading or hearing or interpreting or sifting or verifying).

VII. THE STRUCTURE OF PRIVATE RIGHTS

A. What You Might Modify or Create

1. Contract rights and duties
2. Property rights
3. Liability duties
4. Family law
5. Constitutional rights
6. Labor law
7. Corporate law
8. Criminal law
9. Dispute-resolving institutions other than litigation and courts

B. Why You Might Do It

In recent years, two of the biggest issues drawing the attention of policy analysts and economists interested in legal institutions are the economically efficient incidence of risk—it should fall on the party that can manage it at the lowest social cost—and the costs involved in administering any adjudicative system. Since private-law duties and rights do a lot to allocate risk (e.g., if your product exposes the user to risk and ultimately injury, you may be liable for damages, unless perhaps the user abused or misused it or agreed to assume the risks of use), adjusting laws is sometimes a powerful policy intervention mechanism. Also, much creative thinking has gone into finding ways to bring down the administrative and adjudicative costs.

In addition to these economic matters, there is also concern about compensation for harm. Laws can be changed so as to shift wealth—in some prospectively actuarial sense or in a real present-time sense—among different interests or classes of people.

The wealth-shifting and risk-shifting effects of legal changes may both work in the desired direction, or they may work at cross-purposes. In addition, both may work together with, or at cross-purposes with, the desire to reduce administrative and adjudicative costs.

VIII. THE FRAMEWORK OF ECONOMIC ACTIVITY

A. What You Might Do

1. Encourage competition
2. Encourage concentration
3. Control prices and wages (and profits)
4. Decontrol prices and wages (and profits)
5. Control output levels
6. Decontrol output levels
7. Change tax incentives up or down
8. Provide public jobs
9. Abolish public jobs

B. Why You Might Do It

Supporting more government intervention.   On the supply side, there may be monopoly or oligopoly problems. On the demand side, consumers may be relatively nonmobile or otherwise vulnerable to exploitation—and the same may be true of workers.

Supporting less government intervention.   You might decide that political forces have captured the government administrative apparatus and perverted the intent, or you might decide that the information costs to government entailed in doing the job well are simply too high, or you might think that technology has changed and made an older form of government intervention less appropriate or effective or efficient.

IX. EDUCATION AND CONSULTATION

A. What You Might Do

1. Warn of hazards or dangers
2. Raise consciousness through exhortation or inspiration
3. Provide technical assistance

4. Upgrade skills and competencies

5. Change values

6. Professionalize the providers of a service through training or certification or licensing

B. Why You Might Do It

People may be unaware of a problem or an opportunity. They may be careless or unfeeling. There may be too many untrained or unskilled people in jobs demanding too much responsibility.

X. FINANCING AND CONTRACTING

A. What You Might Do

1. Create a new (governmental) market

2. Abolish an existing (governmental) market

3. Alter reimbursement rates

4. Change the basis for reimbursement (e.g., cost-plus, price per unit, sliding scale dependent on quantity, performance bonuses or penalties)

5. Lease governmentally held resources

6. Alter user fee structure

7. Redesign bidding systems

8. Change contract enforcement methods

9. Furnish loans

10. Guarantee loans

11. Subsidize loans

12. Set up a public enterprise

13. Dismantle a public enterprise

14. "Privatize" a hitherto public enterprise

15. Modify insurance arrangements

16. Change procurement practices

B. Why You Might Do It

Capital and/or insurance markets may be working inefficiently. The governmental contracting and procurement machinery may not be operating well: it may be too rigid, or too corrupt, or too expensive, or too slow.

XI. BUREAUCRATIC AND POLITICAL REFORMS

A. What You Might Do

The number of possibilities is too great to list. It ranges across such activities as reorganizations, replacing top supervisory personnel, improving information systems, and raising wages and salaries.

B. Why You Might Do It

The substantive reasons are too numerous to list. We may note, though, that in many policy contexts there are important political and symbolic considerations for undertaking bureaucratic and political reforms. The political considerations often involve enhancing the power of one social interest or point of view at the expense of another. The symbolic considerations often involve ducking the really hard or impossible problems at the social level in favor of doing something readily seen in a domain over which government appears to have control (that is, its own operations).

SEMANTIC TIPS: A SUMMARY

An unusual feature of this book is the frequent recommendation of semantic tips for using language to make the work of the analyst easier and less vulnerable to pitfalls. It is surprising how easily the right words can improve understanding and the wrong ones can mire us in confusion. Here I collect—and edit slightly in some cases—the principal semantic tips to be found throughout the text.

DEFINING THE PROBLEM

- It often—but not always—helps to think in terms of deficit and excess—for instance, "There are too many homeless people in the United States." To focus on deficit and excess, it often helps to include the word *too* in the problem definition: "too big," "too small," "growing too slowly," "growing too fast." These last two phrases (about growing) remind us that problems deserving our attention don't necessarily exist today but are (at least potentially) in prospect for the future, whether near or distant.
- Most good problem definitions are limited to description. Those that explicitly or implicitly also include a diagnosis of the causes of some problem can be treacherous. Consider, for instance, "In the air pollution area, the problem is that states have not been willing to force motorists to keep their engines tuned up and their exhaust systems in proper order." Suppose, though, that the causal diagnosis is mistaken or misleading (e.g., that states' unwillingness to enforce

engine maintenance routines is *not* in fact a very important cause of air pollution). Because "definition" in some contexts connotes legitimate arbitrariness ("I'll define *justice* to mean . . ."), the causal claims implicit in diagnostic problem definitions can easily escape needed scrutiny.

- Your problem definition should not include an implicit solution introduced by semantic carelessness. Projected solutions must be evaluated empirically and not legitimated merely by definition. Therefore, keep the problem definition stripped down to a mere description, and leave open the search for solutions. *Don't say:* "There is too little shelter for homeless families." This formulation may inadvertently imply that "more shelter" is the best solution and may inhibit you from thinking about ways to prevent families from becoming homeless in the first place. *Try instead:* "There are too many homeless families."

- A tip-off that you're probably smuggling an implicit solution into the problem definition is to hear yourself saying, "Aha, but that's not the real problem; the real problem is . . ." While there are better and worse ways to conceptualize a problem—or to solve a problem—it stretches ordinary usage too much to say that one problem could be "more (or less) real" than another.

ASSEMBLING THE EVIDENCE

- *Data* are facts—or some might say, representations of facts—about the world. Data include all sorts of statistics but go well beyond statistics, too. Data also include, for instance, facts about an agency manager's ability to deal constructively with the press.
- *Information* is data that have meaning, in the sense that they can help you sort the world into different logical or empirical categories. The prevalence of cigarette smoking in five different countries is "data," but these data become "information" when you decide it is interesting to array the countries comparatively (e.g., from lowest to highest prevalence).
- *Evidence* is information that affects the existing beliefs of important people (including yourself) about significant features of the problem you are studying and how it might be solved or mitigated.

Differential prevalence of smoking, for instance, can become evidence bearing on hypotheses about different levels of concern about personal health across countries.

CONSTRUCTING THE ALTERNATIVES

- Always include in your first approach to the problem the alternative "Let present trends continue undisturbed." You need to do this because the world is full of naturally occurring changes, and some of these ongoing changes might mitigate the problem on which you are working. (Note that I am not characterizing this alternative as "Do nothing." It is not possible to "do nothing." Most of the trends in motion will probably persist and alter the problem, whether for better or for worse.)
- The key to simplifying your menu of alternatives, which can become lengthy and complex, is to distinguish between a basic alternative and its variants. The basic element in many policy alternatives is an intervention strategy—such as regulatory enforcement or a subsidy or a tax incentive—that causes people or institutions to change their conduct in some way. But no intervention strategy can stand alone; it must be implemented by some agency or constellation of agencies (perhaps including nonprofit organizations), and it must have a source of financing. Usually the variants on the basic strategy are defined by different methods of implementation and different methods of financing.
- Specifying "alternatives" does not necessarily signify that the policy options are mutually exclusive. Among policy analysts the term *alternative* is used ambiguously. Sometimes it means that choosing one implies foregoing another, and sometimes it means simply one more policy action that might help solve or mitigate some problem, perhaps in conjunction with other alternatives. Sometimes you won't be entirely sure whether two alternatives are or are not mutually exclusive. For instance, the mayor earlier might have promised enough money to either fix potholes or provide homeless shelters (but not both), but you may have made such a great case for both programs that the mayor might decide to increase the budgetary allocation.

SELECTING THE CRITERIA

- Evaluative criteria are *not* used to judge the alternatives, or at least not directly. They are to be applied to the projected outcomes. It is easy to get confused about this point because of a commonsense way of speaking: "Alternative A looks to be the best—therefore let's proceed with it." But this way of speaking ignores a very important step. The complete formulation is "Alternative A will very probably lead to Outcome O_A, which we judge to be the best of the possible outcomes; therefore, we judge Alternative A to be the best." Applying criteria to the evaluation of outcomes and not alternatives makes it possible to remember that we might like O_A a great deal even if, because we lacked sufficient confidence that A would actually lead to O_A, we decided not to choose Alternative A after all. With that judgment on the table, it would be possible to look for other alternatives with a greater likelihood of producing O_A.
- If it is possible to sort your criteria according to whether they refer to values to be maximized, values that stand as constraints, and values that have a more-is-better quality, keep the different statuses of the criteria in mind. Be conscious of them. You can do this with a simple verbal trick: as appropriate, define your criteria as "Maximize such-and-such value"; "Satisfy such-and-such value constraint"; and "Get more of such-and-such value."

PROJECTING THE OUTCOMES

- Assuming for the moment that benefits are uncertain while costs are not, ask yourself these two questions: (1) "Given what I know for sure about the costs of this alternative, what is the minimum help we need to get from Condition X to ensure adequately offsetting benefits?" and (2) "How reasonable is it to believe that Condition X will actually produce that minimum?" Question 1 can also be framed in terms of known benefits and the conditions that would yield minimally acceptable costs.
- Implementation scenarios should be written in the future perfect tense. This encourages concreteness, which is a helpful stimulus to the imagination.

• Analysts are often cautioned to think about *unanticipated conse-quences.* But this term is not appropriate, for it is often used to refer to perfectly anticipatable, though undesirable, side effects.

• A common error that occurs in labeling the "criterion" columns in an outcomes matrix is to fail to indicate what value is at stake and in what dimensions the measurement is being done. For instance, if you are assessing a rental subsidy program, and you enter a plus sign in a column labeled "Landlord/tenant relations," the reader may not know whether you think relations will become more har-monious, more confrontational, less dominated by landlords, less dominated by tenants, or something else. It is not sufficient that your surrounding text makes your intention clear; the matrix label-ing itself must be informative. In my illustrative matrix I did not simply write "Cleanup" or "Cost" or "Time." Within the space con-straints, I tried to indicate the metric and the desired direction it should move in. In many cases it helps to insert *maximize* or *mini-mize* in the criterion label.

CONFRONTING THE TRADE-OFFS

• As economics teaches us, trade-offs occur at the margin. Trade-off analysis tells us something like this: "If we spend an extra X dollars for an extra unit of Service Y, we can get an extra Z units of good outcome." This puts the decision maker in the position to answer the question "Does society (or do you) value Z more or less than X?" and then to follow the obvious implication of the answer (if yes, decide for another unit of Y; if no, don't). A linguistic device to help you keep focused on the margin is frequent use of the word *extra.*

• A common pitfall in confronting trade-offs is to think and speak of the trade-offs as being across *alternatives* rather than across pro-jected *outcomes* (e.g., "trading off twenty foot-patrol officers in the late night hours against a lower-maintenance-cost fleet of police vehicles.") Although there is such a trade-off, you'll see, with a sec-ond's thought, that you can't do anything at all with it. Both alter-natives must first be converted into outcomes before genuine trade-offs can be confronted. Thus, the competing outcomes might be fifty (plus or minus) burglaries per year prevented by the foot-patrol officers versus a savings of $300,000 in fleet maintenance.

- To simplify comparisons and help you focus on key trade-offs, set up benchmarks with one or more "base cases." The most commonly used base case is the set of outcomes you associate with the alternative "letting present trends continue." Other possibly illuminating base cases are these: (1) "The likely outcome if we don't manage to head off what the governor's office [or some other powerful faction] is planning . . ."; (2) "Our ideal set of outcomes if political [or other] conditions were just a bit more favorable . . ."; (3) "Our ideal set of outcomes if we were to weight [some particular] criterion as heavily as we think we ought to . . ."; (4) "The worst-case scenario, which we have to prevent practically at any cost . . ."

INTERVIEWING

- Consider the language of characterization. If an informant says, "Yes, this is a frustrating job," you have to interpret both the nature and intensity of the word *frustrating*, and do so in a way that permits you to calibrate the result against some larger frame or benchmark. This can be done by asking a series of questions designed to do the calibrating. One shortcut is to start by offering up your own characterization and see how the informant reacts to it: "If I had this job, I would find it awfully frustrating, I think." This quickly establishes a benchmark of some kind—"awfully frustrating"—for you and the informant to use. Of course, there is the problem of knowing whether you and your informant mean the same thing by the expression, since your frustration thresholds may differ. But you're off to a good start.

- An improvement on the last example would be to create two such benchmarks, that is, to describe a whole continuum with anchors at both ends, and perhaps a verbal middle point. For example, "Would you say that your reaction to proposal X was extremely skeptical— as I've inferred from what you already have said—or was it relatively favorable . . . or was it maybe 'wait-and-see'?" This sort of approach has the added advantage of respecting virtually any position your informant holds and of communicating your willingness to find anchoring words based in the informant's own history. Or you could anchor one or both ends in what "other people" have supposedly been saying.

DOING "SMART PRACTICES" RESEARCH

- Don't be misled by the *best* in best practices research. Rarely will you have any confidence that some helpful-looking practice is actually the best among all those that are addressed to the same problem or opportunity. The extensive and careful research to document a claim of "best" will almost never have been done. Usually you will be looking for what, more modestly, might be called "good practices."
- I have made a point, in describing each of the supposedly smart practices, of saying that the practice "takes advantage" of something. This is a linguistic device for ensuring that in analyzing how the practice works, we make sure to focus on those aspects of its works that are central—that is, on the fact that the practice aims to exploit, to take advantage of, some latent opportunity for creating value on the cheap.
- In adapting a seeming smart practice from a "source site" for application at a "target site," you want to be rigorous in replicating the logic—the "how"—of the basic mechanism, while leaving maximum flexibility as to the specific means to carry it out. To do this, distinguish between the *functions* involved in getting the mechanism to work and the particular *features* that embody those functions. For instance, in the milestones program, the functions include setting the milestones and verifying the claims of achievement. These actions are part of the defining logic of the practice—they cannot be omitted without changing the very essence of the program. However, exactly what features are chosen to implement these functions or to support the implementation strategy is another matter. With regard to the high-expectations welfare-to-work program, two essential functions are creating a moral climate favoring responsibility and instilling self-confidence that such responsibility can be met. Exactly what design features should be chosen to

implement and support these functions is more open-ended, however.

- Here is a linguistic hint to help you separate features and functions: Functions should be formulated as gerunds, verb-like nouns ending in *ing*—as I did with *setting, verifying, creating,* and *instilling*—while the features that perform these functions can be indicated by pure nouns. An exception to this principle of formulating functional language arises when you really need or want to specify a particular method for carrying out a function. In the milestones case, for instance, you might intentionally refer to a contract as a specific means of defining expectations among the parties and to documents as a means of attesting that the milestones have been met.

REFERENCES

Allison, Graham. 1971. *Essence of Decision: Explaining the Cuban Missile Crisis.* Boston: Little, Brown.

Bardach, Eugene. 1977. *The Implementation Game: What Happens after a Bill Becomes a Law.* Cambridge, Mass.: MIT Press.

———. 1997. Implementing a Paternalist Welfare-to-Work Program. In *The New Paternalism: Supervisory Approaches to Poverty,* ed. Lawrence Mead, 248–278. Washington, D.C.: Brookings Institution.

———. 2004. The Extrapolation Problem: How Can We Learn from the Experience of Others? *Journal of Policy Analysis and Management* 23 (Spring): 205–220.

Barzelay, Michael. 1992. *Breaking through Bureaucracy: A New Vision for Managing in Government.* Berkeley: University of California Press.

Behn, Robert D., and James W. Vaupel. 1982. *Quick Analysis for Busy Decision-Makers.* New York: Basic Books.

Borins, Sandford. 1998. *Innovating with Integrity: How Local Heroes Are Transforming American Government.* Washington, D.C.: Georgetown University Press.

Dery, David. 1984. *Problem Definition in Policy Analysis.* Lawrence: University Press of Kansas.

Farkas, George. 1998. Reading One-to-One: An Intensive Program Serving a Great Many Students While Still Achieving Large Effects. In *Social Programs That Work,* ed. Jonathan Crane, 75–109. New York: Russell Sage Foundation.

Friedman, Lee S. 2002. *Microeconomic Policy Analysis.* Princeton: Princeton University Press.

Glazer, Amihai, and Lawrence S. Rothenberg. 2001. *Why Government Succeeds and Why It Fails.* Cambridge: Harvard University Press.

Greenwood, Peter H., Karyn E. Model, C. Peter Rydell, and James Chiesa. 1995. *Diverting Children from a Life of Crime: Measuring Costs and Benefits.* Santa Monica, Calif.: RAND Corporation.

Lave, Charles A., and James G. March. 1975. *An Introduction to Models in the Social Sciences.* New York: Harper and Row.

Lempert, Robert J., Steven W. Popper, and Steven C. Bankes. 2003. *Shaping the Next One Hundred Years: New Methods for Quantitative, Long-Term Policy Analysis.* Santa Monica, Calif.: RAND Pardee Center.

MacRae, Duncan, Jr., and Dale Whittington. 1997. *Expert Advice for Policy Choice: Analysis and Discourse.* Washington, D.C.: Georgetown University Press.

Moore, Mark H. 1996. *Creating Public Value: Strategic Management in Government.* Cambridge: Harvard University Press.

Morgan, M. Granger, and Max Henrion. 1990. *Uncertainty: A Guide to Dealing with Uncertainty in Quantitative Risk and Policy Analysis.* Cambridge: Cambridge University Press.

Osborne, David, and Ted Gaebler. 1992. *Reinventing Government: How the Entrepreneurial Spirit Is Transforming the Public Sector.* Reading, Mass.: Addison-Wesley.

RAND Corporation. 1994. *Guidelines for Preparing RAND Briefings.* RAND publication no. CP(I)-269. Santa Monica, Calif.: RAND Corporation.

Rosenthal, Stephen R. 1982. *Managing Government Operations.* Boston: Little, Brown.

Salamon, Lester, ed. 2002. *The Tools of Government: A Guide to the New Governance.* New York: Oxford University Press.

Stokey, Edith, and Richard Zeckhauser. 1978. *A Primer for Policy Analysis.* New York: Norton.

Victorio, Andres G. 1995. *Applied Models in Public Policy.* Manila: Ateneo de Manila University.

Weick, Karl E. 1979. *The Social Psychology of Organizing.* 2d ed. Reading, Mass.: Addison-Wesley.

Weimer, David L., and Aidan R. Vining. 2004. *Policy Analysis: Concepts and Practice.* 4th ed. Upper Saddle River, N.J.: Prentice Hall.

Zerbe, Richard O., Jr., and Howard E. McCurdy. 1999. The Failure of Market Failure. *Journal of Policy Analysis and Management* 18, no. 4: 558–578.

INDEX

Note: footnotes and tables are indicated by *n* and *t* after page numbers, respectively